7.95

W9-BVZ-392

BRENNAN MEMORIAL LIBRARY
EDGECLIFF COLLEGE
CINCINNATI, OHIO

PUPPET PLAYS
for
YOUNG PLAYERS

Puppet Plays
for
Young Players

12 royalty-free plays
for hand puppets,
rod puppets or marionettes

by

LEWIS MAHLMANN

AND

DAVID CADWALADER JONES

Publishers   **PLAYS, INC.**   *Boston*

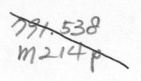

Copyright © 1974 by

LEWIS MAHLMANN AND DAVID CADWALADER JONES

All rights reserved

CAUTION

All material in this volume is fully protected by copyright law. All rights, including motion picture, recitation, television, public reading, radio broadcasting, and rights of translation into foreign languages, are strictly reserved.

NOTICE FOR AMATEUR PRODUCTION

These plays may be produced by schools, clubs, and similar amateur groups without payment of a royalty fee.

NOTICE FOR PROFESSIONAL PRODUCTION

For any form of non-amateur production (professional stage, radio or television), permission must be obtained in writing from the publisher. Inquiries should be addressed to PLAYS, INC., 8 Arlington St., Boston, Massachusetts 02116.

U. S. Library of Congress Cataloging in Publication Data

Mahlmann, Lewis.
  Puppet plays for young players.
  CONTENTS: The magic mushrooms.—The frog prince.—The magic shoes. [etc.]
  1. Puppets and puppet-plays—Juvenile literature. [1. Puppets and puppet-plays] I. Jones, David Cadwalader, joint author. II. Title.
PN1980.M35   791.5'38   73–18421
ISBN 0-8238-0152-7

MANUFACTURED IN THE UNITED STATES OF AMERICA

70434

Contents

Preface

Here are twelve puppet plays that have been written with children of all ages in mind (but can also be performed and enjoyed by adults). They have been successfully produced in a delightful children's park in Oakland, California called Children's Fairyland. There are all kinds of children's tales here, from the simple, original play, *The Magic Mushrooms*, to elaborate productions like *The Wizard of Oz*. Some of these scripts take just a couple of puppeteers, and others require many; all the plays are adaptable to performance by live actors. (There may be some roles, as in the case of animals, where large puppets or actors in masks are preferable, but this is where invention and imagination can have full rein.)

Puppets and puppet shows are as old as time, and are still very popular all over the world. Read through the plays, perhaps with a group of puppeteer friends; then decide which play you want to do, and start right in. The main thing is to have fun. Good luck!

LEWIS MAHLMANN
DAVID CADWALADER JONES

Foreword

Puppetry is a form of art and theatre that has excited me since I first began many years ago.

It is tremendously rewarding as an outlet for many kinds of creative expression. And if you happen to enjoy all forms of art and performance as much as I do, it gives you a chance to try your hand at almost everything.

If you like drawing, painting, sculpting, carpentry, lighting, writing, acting, singing, dancing, or directing, you'll get a chance to do as much as you like of each of these. And if you have a one-person puppet show, you'll do them all.

When you start to do a puppet show, the first question is always what story to do and how to do it with puppets. There are not many good puppet scripts available, so I was delighted to hear that Lewis Mahlmann and David Jones were doing this book.

The scripts are fast-paced and funny, coming from two experienced puppeteers who know what they're doing.

Read through these plays, and, if you've never done a puppet show before, be sure to read the how-to section at the back. Then pick out a script, work hard, and have fun!

JIM HENSON
*Past President, Puppeteers
of America, and creator of
"The Muppets"*

New York, N. Y.

PUPPET PLAYS
for
YOUNG PLAYERS

THE MAGIC MUSHROOMS

Characters

FAIRY
GOBLIN
ELF

Scene One

SETTING: *A forest, near a cave. There are bright red mushrooms with white spots at the base of the trees.*
AT RISE: FAIRY *enters.*

FAIRY: Oh, my! Look at all those beautiful mushrooms! I simply can't resist them. I must have some! (*Begins to eat mushrooms*)

GOBLIN (*From behind the mushrooms*):
Nibble, nibble—sis bam booms!
Who is eating my mushrooms?

FAIRY: Dear, dear! What was that?

GOBLIN (*Jumping out from behind mushrooms*): How dare you eat my mushrooms! They are magic ones and they're very expensive.

FAIRY: I'm so sorry. I didn't know they belonged to anyone.

GOBLIN: Well, it's too late now, so you will have to pay! That will be 300 zlomas, please.

FAIRY: 300 zlomas? My, they are expensive. I only ate one! Well, I'm terribly sorry, but I have no money. I can't pay.

GOBLIN: Good! Then you will have to be my maid. I have a very messy house—and I hate to cook and clean.

1

FAIRY: I certainly will not be your maid! I will find some other mushrooms and pay you back!

GOBLIN: Ha, ha! It's too late! You have already eaten one of the magic mushrooms and now you are under my spell. You will have to do anything I command.

FAIRY: I—I don't believe you.

GOBLIN: Then try to fly away!

FAIRY: All right. Goodbye, you selfish old Goblin. (*She tries to flap her wings.*) I—I can't move! Oh, dear!

GOBLIN: See—what did I tell you? Now, march into that cave over there. (*Points left*) Scrub my floors. Mend my socks and cook my dinner!

FAIRY: Oh, mercy me! I must obey. Some strange power is forcing me to do what you say. (*Both exit left. Curtain.*)

*   *   *

Scene Two

TIME: *Three months later.*

SETTING: *Inside the Goblin's cave. There are a pail and scrub brush on the floor.*

AT RISE: GOBLIN *is taking it easy, lounging in a chair.* FAIRY *is dusting with a feather duster.*

FAIRY: Please, Mr. Goblin, set me free of your spell. I have cleaned your cave for three months now. Won't you let me go?

GOBLIN: I should say not! I've never had such a clean, neat cave or such good meals before.

FAIRY (*Crying*): Oh, boo-hoo!

GOBLIN: There, there. Don't cry. I can't stand seeing fairies cry! I'll give you one chance. If someone offers to take your place, I will let you go.

FAIRY: Oh, no one would ever do that. I'll be trapped here forever. (*Cries*) Boo-hoo!

GOBLIN: Well, don't ever say I didn't give you a chance to break the spell. (*Laughs*) Now I must go out and pick some dew berries for supper. In the meantime you can scrub the walls. I think I saw a spot of dust on them this morning. (*He exits.*)

FAIRY (*Picking up the scrub brush and beginning to scrub wall*): Oh, woe is me! (*Cries*) Boo-hoo . . . (*There is a knock on the door.*) Who's there?

ELF (*Entering*): Hello! Could you tell me how to get to the Elves Club? I'm new in town, and I'm lost.

FAIRY (*Crying*): Boo-hoo! I can't help you. I'm a stranger here, too.

ELF: You are? I thought you lived here. Why are you crying?

FAIRY: Because the wicked goblin who owns this cave has cast a spell on me, and I must do all he says unless someone offers to take my place.

ELF: How terrible! (*Thinks a moment*) Perhaps I can help you. Maybe together we can trick this wicked goblin. Listen—this is what we will do! (*He whispers to her, as curtains close.*)

* * *

Scene Three

TIME: *Later that evening.*
SETTING: *The same as Scene 2.*
AT RISE: GOBLIN *and* FAIRY *sit at dinner table, eating pie.*

GOBLIN: Yum, yum! This is the best dew berry pie I have ever eaten. You are such a good cook. But why aren't you eating?

FAIRY: I'm not hungry.

GOBLIN: Good—then I'll eat the whole pie by myself. (*He gobbles the rest of pie down. There is a knock on the door.*) Who is knocking on my door at this hour? (*He goes to the door.*) Well, what is it? (ELF *enters, carrying a basket of red mushrooms.*)

ELF: Good evening, sir. I am working my way through Elf College. Would you like to buy some mushrooms?

GOBLIN: My, they do look good—almost as good as mine. But, no! I've got enough of my own. Go away!

ELF: Oh, just taste one of these. You will see how good they are.

GOBLIN: Do I have to pay for it?

ELF: No. It's a free sample.

GOBLIN: Good! Gimme, gimme! (*Eats one*) Why, that tastes almost like my magic ones. But not quite as good, of course.

ELF: I can see you don't want to buy any, so I will be on my way. Oh, by the way, who is this lovely creature? (*Pointing to* FAIRY)

GOBLIN: Oh, her? She is my cook and maid.

ELF: A cook and maid! How did you ever find such a lovely one? You must be very clever!

GOBLIN: Oh, I am indeed! She ate one of my magic mushrooms without paying for it, and so she's under my spell. She must do as I say.

ELF: Forever?

GOBLIN: Yes—or until someone offers to take her place. And no one would be foolish enough to do that.

ELF: I don't quite understand. What would a person have to say to take her place?

GOBLIN: My, you are a dull one. He would have to say, "I WILL OFFER TO TAKE THIS FAIRY'S PLACE—TO CLEAN THE CAVE, COOK THE MEALS, AND DO WHATEVER ELSE SHE HAS HAD TO DO TO KEEP THE CAVE NEAT AND CLEAN."

ELF: Ha ha! You foolish Goblin! You have just offered yourself to take her place. That was one of your own mushrooms you ate!

GOBLIN: You tricked me! Oh, I'm so mad! I would hit you, but I don't have time. I must scrub these floors. My, my— look at all that dust. (*He starts scrubbing.*)

ELF: Come, good Fairy. You are now free.

FAIRY: Oh, thank you, sweet Elf. Come. I will help you find the Elves Club. And as for you, you nasty old Goblin, at least you will always have a nice clean house! Goodbye!

GOBLIN: Oh, woe is me. Such a dirty floor—such a dirty floor—(ELF *and* FAIRY *run offstage as* GOBLIN *continues scrubbing. Curtain.*)

THE END

Production Notes

The Magic Mushrooms

Number of Puppets: 3 hand puppets, rod puppets, or marionettes.

Playing Time: 10 minutes.

Description of Puppets: The Fairy has small wings on her back, and wears a filmy dress. Goblin is an ugly puppet with a frightening face. The Elf is a pleasant-looking puppet in a green outfit with pointed hat.

Properties: Pail, scrub brush, pie, feather duster, basket of red mushrooms.

Setting: Scene 1: A forest, near the Goblin's cave. Backdrop shows trees, and red mushrooms with white spots growing at base of trees. Mouth of cave is painted at one side of backdrop. Scenes 2 and 3: The Goblin's cave. Backdrop shows shelves, framed pictures, etc. There are chairs and a table in the room. At one side are scrub brush and pail.

Lighting: No special effects.

THE FROG PRINCE

Adapted from Grimm's fairy tales

Characters

GWENDOLYN, *a spoiled little princess*
MIZARD THE WIZARD
KING GOODFELLOW, *Gwendolyn's father*
PRINCE TAD
FROG
FROG WIZARD

Scene One

SETTING: *The garden of the palace. There is a well just off center stage. A few weeping willow trees are at back. Math book is on bench at side.*

AT RISE: GWENDOLYN *is playing in the garden, bouncing her golden ball.* NOTE: *Put golden rubber ball at end of a piece of straight black coat-hanger wire, and control ball from below or above the stage.*

GWENDOLYN (*In a sing-song fashion*): Bouncy, bouncy, bally. (*Speaks*) It's such a beautiful day. I don't want to study my school work. I'd much rather play bouncy bally. (*Sing-song*) Bouncy, bouncy, bally. (*She throws ball in the air.*)

MIZARD (*Entering*): Oh, there you are, Gwendolyn. Playing bouncy bally? Aren't you learning your arithmetic as your father wants you to?

9

GWENDOLYN: No! I'd much rather play in the garden.

MIZARD: That's right, Princess. Don't you do anything you don't want to do.

GWENDOLYN: I won't. (*She bounces ball again.*) Bouncy, bouncy, bally.

KING (*From offstage*): Gwendolyn! Oh, Gwendolyn, my child!

MIZARD: Your father's coming. You'd better hide that golden ball and pretend you're studying. Here's your arithmetic book. (*He hands it to her.*)

GWENDOLYN: I'll put this golden ball behind the well. He'll never see it there. (*She hides ball behind well.*)

MIZARD: Here's the book. (*She takes it.*) Heh-heh! (*To himself*) She has it upside down. (*He exits.* KING *enters from other side of stage.*)

GWENDOLYN (*Reading from book*): Two plus two equals . . . seven. Three plus two equals . . . nine.

KING (*To himself*): Oh, isn't that sweet! Gwendolyn is studying her new math. I never could understand those figures myself. She is such a good girl. (KING *turns away and* GWENDOLYN *sticks her tongue out at him.*)

GWENDOLYN (*Jeering*): Yah-h-h!

KING (*Turning*): What did you say, dear?

GWENDOLYN: Oh, I was just stretching, Papa. I'm so tired from studying so hard.

KING: That's my good girl. Oh, by the way—did you see a golden ball? There seems to be one missing from the treasury.

GWENDOLYN: Oh, no, Daddy. What would I be doing with a golden ball?

KING: Well, I just thought I'd ask. Now, don't be late for supper.

GWENDOLYN: I won't, Daddy. (KING *exits.*) I won't study

my books. (*She throws book into well.*) That's for you,
Mr. Arithmetic. I won't read any book, except maybe a
comic book.

MIZARD (*Re-entering*): Has the King gone yet?

GWENDOLYN: Yes.

MIZARD: Fine. Now—what'll we do today?

GWENDOLYN: Let's play ball. (*She gets golden ball from
behind well.*)

MIZARD: Play ball? (*Laughs*) Ho ho! I haven't played ball
since I was knee-high to a toad. How do you play that?

GWENDOLYN: It's easy. Just stand over there. (*Points to
well*)

MIZARD: Over here? (*He moves backward to the edge of
the well.*)

GWENDOLYN: That's good. Now catch! (*She throws ball to
him. It knocks him backward into well. Ball lands on stage
and not in well.*)

MIZARD (*From well*): Help! Hel-l-l-p! I'm drowning. Help!
Save me!

GWENDOLYN (*Picking up ball*): Oh, dear, my golden ball
almost fell into the well.

MIZARD (*From well*): Hel-l-l-p!

GWENDOLYN (*In a sing-song fashion*):
    Mizard's in the well.
    Who pushed him in?
    Little Tommy Tin.
    Who'll pull him out?
    Not me! (*She laughs.*)
    Bouncy, bouncy, bally . . .
    (*She exits, singing and bouncing ball.*)

MIZARD (*From well*): Help! Someone! Anybody! Get me
out of here! (PRINCE *enters.*)

PRINCE: Did I hear somebody yell for help? Where are you?

MIZARD (*From well*): In the well. Get me out! ·

PRINCE (*Rushing to well*): Here! Give me your hand! Now —up you come! (PRINCE *reaches into well and with much effort pulls* MIZARD *out.* MIZARD's *robe is wet and it has shrunk.*)

MIZARD (*Coughing*): I'm half drowned. Who are you, anyway?

PRINCE: I'm Prince Tad. (*Laughs*) Look at your clothes! They've shrunk.

MIZARD: Why did you come here?

PRINCE: I've come to meet Princess Gwendolyn. I hope to make her my wife one day.

MIZARD: Meet the Princess, huh? Laugh at me, huh? You'll meet the Princess, all right. But not like that. I'm going to turn you into a frog.

PRINCE: Keep away from me, you old fake. (PRINCE *backs behind well.*)

MIZARD: A fake, am I? I'll fix you! (*Chants*)
> Flip, flop, from the top,
> Into a frog you cannot stop.
> Until she does good deeds three,
> You, an ugly frog shall be.

(PRINCE *sinks behind well and* FROG *appears on well.*)

FROG: Grr-up! Grr-up!

MIZARD (*Throwing* FROG *into well*): Now stay down there in the well where you belong. (*He laughs.*)

GWENDOLYN (*Entering, bouncing her ball*): Bouncy, bouncy, bally. Bouncy, bouncy—Mizard! How did you get out of the well?

MIZARD: I'm a wizard and so I wished myself out—that's how.

GWENDOLYN: Play ball with me again.

MIZARD: Oh, play ball with the frogs in the well. (*He exits.*)

GWENDOLYN (*Calling after him*): You come back here! (*Shrugs*) Well—I'll just play ball by myself, then. Bouncy, bouncy, bally. (*Throws ball up and catches it*) Bouncy, bouncy, bally. Bouncy, bouncy— (*Ball falls into well.*) Oh! My beautiful golden ball. It fell into the well. Oh, no! How am I going to get it out? My poor beautiful ball. (*She cries.*) Boo hoo! I wish there were someone who would get my ball for me. (*She hides her face in her hands, crying, as* FROG *appears on edge of well.*)

FROG: Princess Gwendolyn!

GWENDOLYN (*Looking up*): Who said that?

FROG: It's your froggie, Gwendolyn.

GWENDOLYN: You're not my froggie! Get back in the well. (*She pushes him in. To herself*) Oh—now maybe he could get my golden ball for me. (*Calls into well, sweetly*) Yoo-hoo! Froggie, dear! Oh, Froggie!

FROG (*Appearing*): Yes, my Gwendolyn?

GWENDOLYN: I seem to have dropped my beautiful golden ball down your well and I can't get it out. Would you get it for me, Froggie?

FROG: I am eager to do your bidding—but first you must do three favors for me.

GWENDOLYN: What are the three favors I must do?

FROG: Well—come closer—first you must let me eat from your golden plate.

GWENDOLYN: Well, really!

FROG: Second—come a little closer—you must let me sleep at the foot of your bed tonight.

GWENDOLYN: Well, I never!

FROG: Third—come still closer—you must give me a kiss.

GWENDOLYN: Well, of all the nerve! Never!

FROG: Then I can't help you get your ball. (*He disappears again.*)

GWENDOLYN (*Calling*): Yoo-hoo! Froggie! All right. I'll do it.

FROG (*Appearing*): Then I'll get your ball for you. (*He goes back into well.*)

GWENDOLYN: Well! If he thinks I'm going to do those things for him, he has another guess coming. It would be all right if he were a handsome prince, but a frog? Never!

FROG (*Appearing with ball*): Here's your golden ball, Gwendolyn. Now don't forget your promises.

GWENDOLYN: If you think I'm going to keep my promises to an ugly old frog, you are wrong. (*She pushes him back into well.*) Now stay down there where you belong. Kiss a frog? *Never!* (*She exits, singing*) Bouncy, bouncy, bally! (*Curtain.*)

*   *   *

Scene Two

TIME: *Later that day.*

SETTING: *Dining room in the palace. There is a fancy table set for two with delicious-looking food on it. King's throne has been pulled up to the table. There is a little fancy chair for Gwendolyn.*

AT RISE: GWENDOLYN *enters, still bouncing her golden ball.*

GWENDOLYN: Bouncy, bouncy, bally! Bouncy, bouncy, bally. Oh—look at that terrible table and all those awful things to eat. Filet mignon—asparagus—and raspberry mousse. Ugh! I just won't eat, that's all. I won't eat anything! I don't want to.

KING (*Entering*): Oh, there you are, Gwendolyn, my sweet

little girl. It's time for supper. Doesn't that look delicious? (*He sits at table.*)

GWENDOLYN: No! It looks awful! I hate all that old food.

KING: But, Gwendolyn, it's good for you.

GWENDOLYN: I know what's good for me. I want candy, cake, cookies, and ice cream.

KING: But, Gwendolyn. . . . (*There is a knock on door offstage.*) There seems to be someone at the front door of the castle.

GWENDOLYN: I don't hear anyone, Papa.

KING: I'm sure I heard a knocking. (*Gets up, starts off*)

GWENDOLYN (*Holding his cape as he tries to walk*): There's no one there, Papa.

KING (*Breaking away*): I'll just go see who it is. (*He exits.*)

GWENDOLYN: It's probably that terrible frog. Ugh! I'll just pretend I don't know him. (*She turns away.*)

KING (*Re-entering with* FROG): Well, lookee here! It's a little froggie, Gwendolyn! He says he knows you.

GWENDOLYN: I've never seen him before in my whole life.

KING: And he says you promised him he could eat from your golden plate.

GWENDOLYN: He's a big, fat liar!

KING (*Shocked*): Now Gwendolyn! Frogs that talk don't usually tell fibs, now do they? We will just put him in my chair . . . (*Places* FROG *on throne*) Now he can reach your plate. Can't you, Mr. Frog?

FROG: Did you forget your promise, Gwendolyn?

KING: I'll go get him a napkin. (KING *exits.*)

FROG (*Jumping on table and beginning to eat*): Oh, Princess, this is delicious.

GWENDOLYN: Well, if you like it so much—eat it all. (*She upsets plate on top of* FROG's *head.*)

FROG (*Coughing and spluttering*): Hm-m-m-m—delicious.

KING (*Entering*): Here's his napkin—Oh! I see he is done.

FROG: Don't forget tonight, Princess.

KING: What's happening tonight? Is there going to be a party? I just *love* parties.

GWENDOLYN: He's done now, Papa. I'll show the sweet little froggie to the door. (*She drags* FROG *from table and exits quickly with him.*)

KING (*To audience*): Isn't she sweet? She just loves animals. (*He exits. Loud noise of door slamming is heard from off-stage.*)

GWENDOLYN (*From offstage; shouting*): And stay out! (*She enters.*) Well! If he thinks I'm going to let him sleep in my bedroom tonight, he has another think coming. Sleep near a frog? Never! (*She exits. Curtain.*)

*   *   *

Scene Three

SETTING: *Gwendolyn's bedroom. There is a large open window center stage. The bed is down left.*

AT RISE: GWENDOLYN *is in bed, wearing a nightgown, tossing golden ball in air.*

GWENDOLYN (*In a tired voice*): Bouncy, bouncy, bally! (*Yawns*) Bouncy, bouncy, bally—(*Yawns again*) Oh, I just know that I'll dream of slimy things like snakes and frogs tonight. But one good thing! I've locked all the doors so he can't get in. (*She yawns and falls asleep.*)

FROG (*Calling from offstage*): Gwendolyn! My Gwendolyn!

GWENDOLYN (*Sitting up*): What was that?

FROG (*Appearing at window*): Gwendolyn! It's your frog-gie, Gwendolyn!

GWENDOLYN: He's come back!

FROG (*Jumping in and jumping onto foot of bed*): Did you forget your second promise?

GWENDOLYN: Get out of here! Help! Help! Someone help me! (*She jumps out of bed and runs to window.*) Hel-l-l-p!

KING (*Entering, in his nightshirt*): Gwendolyn, what's wrong?

GWENDOLYN: He's back, Daddy!

KING: Who? (*He sees* FROG.) Oh, hello, Froggie! Gwendolyn, here's your froggie again!

GWENDOLYN: Ugh!

KING: You didn't promise him something else, did you?

GWENDOLYN: No!

KING: Now, Gwendolyn. It isn't character-building if we don't keep our promises.

GWENDOLYN: Well—I said he could sleep at the foot of my bed tonight, but . . .

KING: Then sleep here he will. It's only for one night. Now back to bed with you. You will catch your death of cold. (*He ushers her back to bed.*) Now sleep tight. (*He kisses her on forehead.*) And good night to you, Mr. Froggie. (*Pats him on head*) Strange . . . very strange . . . (*He exits.*)

GWENDOLYN: Just you wait, Mr. Slimy. Just—you—wait! (*Curtain*)

* * *

Scene Four

SETTING: *The palace garden, the same as Scene 1.*

AT RISE: FROG *jumps out of well and hides behind it, just as* MIZARD *enters, carrying a metal lid. He covers well with lid.*

MIZARD: The Prince won't meet the Princess now! (*Cackles*)

GWENDOLYN (*Entering*): Mizard, what are you doing?

MIZARD: Your frog won't get out this time. I've put a heavy metal lid on the well. Now I'll get a big stone and put it on the lid to hold it down. (*He exits.*)

GWENDOLYN: Happy day! (*Sings to tune of "London Bridge Is Falling Down"*)

>Now we're rid of Mister Frog,
>Mister Frog, Mister Frog,
>Now I'll do just as I please,
>I'm free of him.

(*Speaks*) I'm free! Hooray!

FROG (*Jumping out from behind well*): Gwendolyn! My sweet Gwendolyn!

GWENDOLYN: Who said that? (*Turns and sees* FROG *behind her*) Oh, no! (*Runs around stage with* FROG *chasing her*) Get away from me! Get away!

FROG: Did you forget your last promise, Gwendolyn?

GWENDOLYN: Help! Help! (*She falls.*) Ooops! I tripped.

FROG: Gwendolyn! (*He gives her a big kiss.*)

GWENDOLYN: Ecch! Ecch! Help! I've been kissed by a frog! (FROG *goes behind well.*) Help! (*She runs offstage.*)

FROG (*From behind well*): Come back, Gwendolyn! (PRINCE TAD *steps out from behind well.*)

PRINCE: Come back, Gwendolyn! (*He discovers that he is*

no longer a frog.) Why, look at me! I'm no longer a frog. I'm a prince again!

MIZARD (*Entering*): Oh! You've broken the spell, have you? We'll see about that. I'll put you under another spell. (*Thinks a moment*) Now how does it go? Flop, flip? (*While* MIZARD *is thinking and reciting,* PRINCE *takes lid from well and holds it like a shield in front of himself.* MIZARD, *still mumbling, crosses to stand behind well.*) Now I remember! (*Recites*)

> Flip, flop, from the top,
> Into a frog, you cannot stop.
> So turn into a frog once more,
> And remain a frog forevermore.

Oh, no! What have I done? My reflection—in the lid—I've cast the spell upon myself! Oh, no! (*He falls down behind well, and in an instant* FROG WIZARD *leaps out from behind well.*)

FROG WIZARD: Brr-up! Brr-up!

PRINCE: Mizard the Wizard turned himself into a frog! Well, what do you know?

GWENDOLYN (*Re-entering*): Mizard, where are you? (*She sees* PRINCE TAD) Oh! Who are you?

PRINCE: I was the frog who ate from your golden plate, slept at the foot of your bed, and gave you a kiss a moment ago. Evil Mizard the Wizard put me under a spell, and turned me into a frog. Only you could free me from the spell. I am really Prince Tad, and I have come to make you my wife.

GWENDOLYN: Well, I think I should have something to say about that. But I'm glad you're not a frog anymore. By the way, where is Mizard the Wizard?

PRINCE: There he is, on the well. (*Points to* FROG WIZARD)

GWENDOLYN: That doesn't look like Mizard—it looks like an awful old frog, and I'm sick of them. (*She picks up* FROG WIZARD *and drops him into well, then calls after him.*) Stay there and don't come up again, do you hear? (*To* PRINCE) Now, if you were a proper prince, you would have brought me a present. All true princes bring princesses presents. You should give me what I deserve.

PRINCE: I have a present for you. I have brought you what you deserve. Come here, Gwendolyn.

GWENDOLYN (*Curiously; approaching him*): What is it? Let me have it!

PRINCE: Here it is. (*He puts her over well and spanks her.*) A good spanking!

GWENDOLYN: Stop! Help! (*She wails.*) Oh-h-h-h!

PRINCE: You will learn your spelling, your arithmetic, be good to your papa, and be good to others, too. (*Spanks her again*)

GWENDOLYN: Yes! I'll be good. (*Wails again*) Oh-h-h! Yes, my prince!

PRINCE: Your Prince Tad, forevermore. (*He stops spanking her.*)

GWENDOLYN (*Standing*): My Prince Tad forevermore.

PRINCE: We will be happy together and rule wisely, won't we?

GWENDOLYN: Yes—yes! I'll be good, my prince—my Frog Prince! (*They kiss and exit together. Curtain*)

THE END

70434

Production Notes

THE FROG PRINCE

Number of Puppets: 6 hand puppets or marionettes.

Playing Time: 20 minutes.

Description of Puppets: Gwendolyn wears a long gown, and
   a small crown on top of her hair (which may be made of
   gold fringe). Mizard the Wizard wears a turban and long
   robes. He has an earring in one ear. After he falls into well,
   he wears a shorter robe made of shiny fabric to look as if
   it is wet and has shrunk. King Goodfellow is chubby. He
   wears an elegant crown, and a cape. Prince Tad wears a
   beret with a feather, and a jacket with a short cape. Frog
   may have crossed eyes. Frog Wizard has a small turban
   and earring to look like Mizard.

Properties: Golden ball on the end of heavy wire; math book;
   dishes of food; plates; napkin; lid for well.

Setting: Scenes 1 and 4: Palace garden. Well is just off center
   stage. A few weeping willow trees are at back. Bench is
   at one side. Scene 2: The dining room of the palace. There
   is a fancy table set for two at center, with King's throne
   at one end and small chair for Gwendolyn at other. Scene
   3: Gwendolyn's bedroom. A large open window is at center stage. Bed is down left.

Lighting: No special effects.

THE MAGIC SHOES

Characters

NARRATOR
JAN SCHUHMACHER, *the shoemaker*
KAY, *his wife*
FRAU UNTERMEIER
MICK ⎫ *two elves*
MIKE ⎭
CINDERELLA
PRINCE CHARMING
PUSS-IN-BOOTS
THE GOOD WITCH OF THE NORTH
OFFSTAGE VOICE

Scene One

SETTING: *The shoemaker's shop, a simple, bare room, with half-timbered walls. There is a workbench at one side, with a hammer and pieces of leather lying on it. Painted on the backdrop are the front window of the shop (with the word* SHOES *lettered on it backward), a grandfather clock, and a set of shelves with shoes on them. A real curtain hangs over the shelves.*

AT RISE: JAN, *the shoemaker, is sitting at his workbench.*

JAN: Oh, how am I to tell my wife the bad news? This is my last piece of leather. Tomorrow I will make a pair of shoes from it, and then (*Groans*)—oh-h-h—and then—we will be penniless! (KAY *enters, with a bowl.*)

23

KAY: Here is some soup, *liebchen*. You must eat. You are getting so thin and pale.

JAN: Ja—but I am not hungry. You eat it, Kay.

KAY: But, Jan, you must eat something.

JAN: Who can eat? I am so tired, and I have used my last piece of leather. There is only enough for one pair of shoes. Tomorrow I will sew them, and when they are sold, I do not know what will become of us.

KAY: Do not worry. Something nice will happen soon for us. My horoscope said so.

JAN: Ah, my dear Kay, you are such a dreamer! I am afraid I have failed you. Come, let us go to bed. Tomorrow I must put the shop up for sale, and then—oh, dear, oh, dear. (*They exit. Curtain.*)

*   *   *

Scene Two

TIME: *The next morning.*

SETTING: *The same as Scene 1.*

AT RISE: *There is a pair of women's shoes on workbench. The stage is empty.*

NARRATOR: The next morning, the shoemaker got up early and went to his workbench, ready to make the shoes. (JAN *enters and crosses to workbench.*)

JAN (*Seeing shoes; surprised*): What's this? *Was ist los?* The shoes—they are already made! (*Calling*) Kay! Come here, quickly!

KAY (*From offstage*): *Ja?* What is the matter? (*She enters.*)

JAN: Look! The shoes! They have already been sewn. And

with not one bad stitch in them! When did you do it? You must have stayed up all night!

KAY: But—I did not do it! I slept soundly all night.

JAN: Then who could have sewn them? I have never seen a pair of shoes so well made. They are perfect.

KAY: Here comes Frau Untermeier from the orphanage. I wonder what she wants? (FRAU UNTERMEIER *enters*.)

FRAU: Good day, good day, Herr Schuhmacher. Have you heard the bad news? The orphanage burned down last night.

JAN: Oh, my! And the children?

FRAU: All saved. But terribly frightened. They are staying at the old inn right now, but I don't know what's to become of them. We don't have enough money to build a new orphanage. It's too bad they can't live in one of your shoes! (*Laughs*) And speaking of shoes, may I see that lovely pair of shoes on your workbench? (*Crosses to workbench and inspects shoes*) Oh, they're just beautiful. And just right for my new gown. I must have them. How much are they?

JAN: Why—um—oh, 200 pfennigs?

FRAU: My, my. You are much too reasonable. (*Gives him coins*) Here are 400, and well worth it, too. I must be running along now. Wait until the girls see my shoes. They'll be so envious. (*Exits, with shoes*)

JAN: 400 pfennigs—I never got so much for shoes before! Now I can buy some more leather and make two pairs of shoes.

KAY: And we will still have some money left for food.

JAN: Maybe your horoscope was right after all! (*Curtain*)

*   *   *

Scene Three

TIME: *A day later.*
SETTING: *The same as Scene 1.*
AT RISE: *There are a pair of red slippers and a small pair of boots on the workbench.*

NARRATOR: That night, before he went to bed, the shoe-maker cut out two pairs of shoes from the leather he had bought and left them on his workbench, all ready to be sewn. The next morning. . . . (JAN *enters.*)

JAN: Well, now to get busy and make those shoes. (*He sees the finished shoes on the bench.*) What! It cannot be! They are already made again! (*Calling*) Kay! Kay! Come quickly! (KAY *hurries in.*)

KAY: What is it, dear?

JAN: Look! More shoes. Even more beautiful than the first pair. And not a bad stitch in any of them.

KAY: Oh, but look . . . the boots are so small. Even a child could not wear them. (PUSS-IN-BOOTS *enters, without boots.*)

PUSS: Meow! Good day, Herr Schuhmacher.

JAN: Upon my word! A talking cat.

PUSS: You don't by any chance have a pair of boots that would fit me, do you? I must go out to seek a fortune for my master, and I need some boots to wear.

KAY (*To* JAN): You don't suppose . . .

JAN: Why, yes. (*Pointing to boots*) I think these boots will fit you just fine!

PUSS: Good. (*Examines boots*) Why, they are just my size! I'm afraid I haven't much to give you for them, but if you will let me have them I can promise you some important customers in the future. I expect to have many influential friends at the palace.

JAN: Very well. You may have them, for I'm afraid they wouldn't fit many other customers.

PUSS: I assure you, you won't regret this. (PUSS *picks up boots.*) Good day. (*He turns to exit and bumps into* THE GOOD WITCH OF THE NORTH *as she enters.*) Oh, excuse me, ma'am. (PUSS *exits.*)

WITCH: Those shoes—those ruby-red slippers on your workshop bench. I must have them! I am leaving for Oz tomorrow, and they are just what I need for my trip.

JAN: Would you like to try them on?

WITCH: No need . . . no need. I know they'll fit. Here! (*Hands him a gold coin*) All that I have is this gold coin.

JAN: But I have no change for that.

WITCH: Oh, that's all right. I feel generous today. Don't bother to wrap them. (*She picks up shoes*) Good day. Such beautiful shoes—such beautiful shoes! (*She exits.*)

JAN (*To* KAY): Look, *liebchen!* (*Shows coin to her*) Now we have enough money to buy leather, and food for a whole month.

KAY: Oh, how lucky we are! If we only had children to share our happiness.

JAN: Yes, but we can't have everything, I suppose. Come to bed. Tomorrow will be a big day. I will buy still more leather.

KAY: And some cornmeal and bacon . . .

JAN: And new tools. . . .

KAY: And a new tablecloth. . . .

JAN: And a new sign for my shop. . . .

KAY (*As they start out*): And new curtains. . . . (*They exit. Clock is heard striking twelve.* MICK *and* MIKE, *two elves, enter.*)

MICK: Did you see their faces, Mike? They looked so happy!

MIKE: Yes. And wait until they see the shoes we'll have ready for them tomorrow!

MICK *and* MIKE (*Singing to tune of "Brother, Come and Dance with Me" from "Hansel and Gretel"*):

> Mend and hammer, stitch and sew,
> We're the shoe elves, don't you know.
> Making shoes for people's feet,
> Sewing stitches, nice and neat.
>
> Oh, you're bound our shoes to like!
> We're the shoe elves, Mick and Mike.
> Look and see—and no fee—
> Dancing all about with glee!

(*They go to workbench and pantomime making shoes.*)

MIKE: Pass the hammer!

MICK: Quick—more nails!

MIKE: There. That's done! (*Holds up a pair of glass slippers*) A beautiful pair of glass slippers!

MICK: Wait until the shoemaker and his wife see these shoes! (MICK *pulls curtain aside, revealing many pairs of new shoes on shelves. Elves begin to hum "Brother, Come and Dance with Me" and elves and glass slippers dance. When dance is over, slippers hop onto workbench. See Production Notes.*)

MIKE: We'd better leave now, before they wake up.

MICK: Yes. We still have that straw to spin into gold for Uncle Rumple.

MIKE: Good night, little shoes!

MICK: Good night, old clock! (*Clock strikes one and elves hurry out.* JAN *enters.*)

JAN: What was that? I thought I heard a noise in here. (*Sees glass slippers on workbench*) Oh, my. It's happened again!

KAY (*From offstage*): What was it, dear?

JAN: Come out here. (*She enters.*) I didn't see anyone, but look—more shoes!

KAY (*Going to workbench*): Oh—these charming glass slippers!

JAN: No one will want to buy them. They are too fragile. (*Sound of trumpet fanfare is heard from offstage.*)

KAY: What was that?

OFFSTAGE VOICE: Make way for his highness, Prince Charming!

JAN: Now, I wonder what the Prince is doing in town? (CINDERELLA *enters.*)

CINDERELLA (*Crying*): Oh, boo-hoo! I hope you can help me. You're my last hope.

JAN: Why, my poor dear niece, Cinderella. What is the matter?

KAY: Are your stepsisters being mean to you again?

CINDERELLA: Oh, no. It's not that—it's . . . it's. . . . (*Weeps*)

JAN: What is it, Cinderella? Tell us!

CINDERELLA: The Prince is searching each home to find the girl who lost her glass slipper at his ball last night. I was the one who lost it.

KAY: Then you should be happy.

CINDERELLA: But he wants to see if the slippers match, and —and—

JAN: Yes? Yes?

CINDERELLA: And I dropped mine and it broke into a thousand pieces. (*Weeps*)

KAY: Jan—you don't suppose. . . .

JAN: Why, yes. (*To* CINDERELLA) Don't cry, Cinderella. I have just the thing for you. (*He shows her glass slippers.*)

CINDERELLA: Why, they're exactly the same as mine! I'll only need one. I left the right one, so the left one is right for me.

JAN: What was that again?

CINDERELLA (*Taking left shoe*): This is the one I'll need. And thank you, Uncle Jan. You saved my life.

JAN: Well, a stitch in time—

KAY: Come back again soon, for pumpkin pie.

CINDERELLA: Goodbye! (*She exits.*)

JAN: Such a sweet girl.

KAY: Yes, but I do wish she would be more tidy. She had ashes all over her dress.

OFFSTAGE VOICE: His majesty, the Prince! (PRINCE CHARMING *enters.*)

JAN (*Bowing deeply*): Your Highness.

PRINCE: Good day, shoemaker.

KAY: Why have you come here?

PRINCE: Quite frankly, I was hoping you could help me. You see, I was supposed to go around town, checking each girl's foot to see if it would fit the glass slipper left at my ball last night.

JAN: Yes, we know, but—

PRINCE: Well, I dropped the slipper.

JAN: And it broke into a thousand pieces.

PRINCE: Yes—but how did you know? Anyway—I thought maybe you might have a spare glass slipper lying around. I've already committed myself, you see.

JAN: It just so happens—

KAY: Here! (*Points to remaining glass slipper*)

PRINCE: Why—it looks exactly the same as the one I broke. And the right foot, too!

JAN (*Nodding*): Yes, we know.

PRINCE: What was that?

JAN: Er—we know you will be happy with it.

PRINCE: Those other shoes on your shelves—magnificent! I never saw such shoes before. I will buy them all. And for being such a help to me—and such a marvelous shoemaker —I hereby appoint you royal shoemaker to the King's castle. Will one million pfennigs a week be enough for you?

JAN: Oh! Why, more than enough, Your Highness.

PRINCE: So be it. Good day to you both. (PRINCE *exits.*)

KAY: Oh, Jan. We will be so rich!

JAN: Maybe we can share our luck with others. Let us stay up late tonight and try to find out who has been making our shoes for us. Maybe we can do something for them, too.

KAY: We'll hide behind the door. (*They exit. The clock strikes twelve.* MICK *and* MIKE *enter.*)

MIKE: Br-r-r! It certainly is cold outside.

MICK: Yes. It's good to be inside where there is a warm fire.

MIKE: Let's get to work. We don't have much time, you know. (*They hum their song and hammer away, producing more shoes, which they leave on workbench.*) There. All done.

MICK: Don't forget to take some leather and nails. You know what we have to make next.

MIKE: Oh, yes. Won't they be surprised!

MICK: Better bring a ladder, too. There is one outside.

MIKE: We're off. (*They exit.* JAN *and* KAY *re-enter.*)

JAN: Can I believe my eyes?

KAY: Oh, those sweet little elves. If only we had two sweet children like them!

JAN: Maybe we could do something for them. Hmmm. . . . I wonder why they took a ladder?

KAY: They did look so cold! Maybe I could knit each of them a warm red scarf with little bells on the ends.

JAN: Oh, that would be nice. And I'll make them some new red shoes for their tiny feet.

KAY: Come! If we start now, we can be finished before morning. (*They bustle about, as curtains close.*)

*   *   *

Scene Four

TIME: *The following day.*
SETTING: *The same as Scene 1.*
AT RISE: *The stage is empty.*

NARRATOR: And so, the shoemaker and his wife worked far into the early hours of the morning, and then left the newly made scarves and shoes on their doorstep, for the little elves. When they awoke, the scarves and shoes were gone. (JAN *and* KAY *enter.*) Later that day. . . .

JAN: Look, Kay. Here comes Frau Untermeier again. (FRAU UNTERMEIER *enters.*)

FRAU: Hello, hello! What a wonderful thing you have done. It is simply marvelous. The children love it.

JAN: Why, what are you talking about?

FRAU: The new orphanage, of course. How did you ever think of it?

JAN: But I—I—

FRAU: Now, now. Don't be modest. Imagine, building an orphanage in the shape of a shoe! Why, you are the only one around that could have built it; and every stitch is perfect.

JAN: The orphanage—in the shape of a shoe?

FRAU: Yes, and already the children have made up a little verse about me. Now, how did that go? Oh, yes! (*Recites*)
There was an old woman who lived in a shoe.
She had so many children she didn't know what to do.
Catchy, isn't it?

JAN: Why, yes.

FRAU: Oh, everything would be perfect now, if only *it* hadn't happened!

JAN: It?

KAY: It?

FRAU: Yes. We had just enough room in the shoe for all the children, and then, just a few minutes ago someone left a basket on our doorstep with two of the most charming little baby boys in it! And we simply have no room for them. If only we could find someone who would take them in!

KAY: Jan?

JAN: Kay?

FRAU: It's the oddest thing—they were both wearing the cutest little red scarves with bells on them, and tiny little red shoes. And they both have the sweetest little elfin grins. You wouldn't happen to know anyone who would want to adopt them, would you?

KAY: Oh, Jan. . . .

JAN: Oh, Kay!

NARRATOR: And everything was O.K. and the *four* of them lived happily ever after! (*Curtain*)

THE END

Production Notes

THE MAGIC SHOES

Number of Puppets: 9 hand puppets or marionettes.

Playing Time: 15 minutes.

Description of Puppets: Jan, the shoemaker, wears a shoe-maker's apron with a plain shirt and patched trousers. Kay, his wife, wears a mob cap and apron over a plain skirt and blouse. Mick and Mike, the elves, are very small, bare-footed (if they are marionettes), and wear little pointed hats. Frau Untermeier has a shawl around her shoulders, a full skirt, and a perky hat on her head. She carries a shopping basket into which she puts her new shoes. Cinderella, Prince Charming, Puss-in-Boots and the Good Witch of the North look just as the story books show them.

Properties: Bowl; silver coins; gold coins; small pairs of women's shoes, ruby-red shoes, small boots, and glass slippers. For a puppet show, put rods on slippers so that they can dance. For a marionette show, string the shoes and weight them.

Setting: The shoemaker's shop, a simple, bare room, with quaint half-timbered walls. There is a workbench at one side of stage (the playboard may be used as the work-bench, if it is a hand puppet stage), with a hammer on it, and pieces of leather (or brown paper). Painted on the backdrop are the front window of the shop (with the word SHOES lettered on it backward), a grandfather clock, and a set of shelves with shoes on them. A real curtain hangs

over the shelves, on rings, so that it can be pulled back.
Lighting: No special effects.
Sound: Offstage voice, and trumpet fanfare, as indicated in
text.

WHY THE SEA IS SALT

Characters

SHARKIE ⎫
FLIPPER ⎬ *fish*
CHARLIE ⎭
GILLIE, *a little boy fish*
GRANNY, *his grandmother*
OLIVER, *a poor man*
MARTHA, *his wife*
MERVIN, *his rich, greedy brother*
DWARF

Scene One

TIME: *The present.*
SETTING: *The ocean floor. This scene is played behind a sea scrim.*
AT RISE: *Four little fish,* SHARKIE, FLIPPER, CHARLIE *and* GILLIE, *swim in, in front of scrim.*

GILLIE: 'Bye, Sharkie. 'Bye, Flipper. 'Bye, Charlie. See you guys in school tomorrow. (SHARKIE, FLIPPER *and* CHARLIE *swim off.* GILLIE *calls.*) Granny—I'm home! (GRANNY *swims in.*)
GRANNY: My, you're home early, Gillie. You weren't naughty at fish school today, were you?
GILLIE: Oh, no, Granny. Miss Trout let us out early on porpoise today.
GRANNY: That's nice. Just so you weren't playing hookie.

37

You know what a nasty word that is! Now, tell Granny
—what did you learn in school today?

GILLIE: Well, Mr. Bass, our gym teacher, taught us how to
catch a fly. And Miss Trout taught us something very silly.
I think she was only kidding, though.

GRANNY: She wouldn't do that, Gillie. What did she say?

GILLIE: She said that the sea was salt! She *was* kidding, wasn't
she?

GRANNY: Oh, my, no! What she said is very true.

GILLIE: But how can that be, Granny?

GRANNY: Well, it's a very long story, child. Swim over here,
closer to Granny, and I'll explain to you how it all happened. (GILLIE *swims over to* GRANNY.) You see, a long
time ago there lived on the dry part of Earth a poor tailor
and his wife. They were good people—not like that kind
that hunt us in these waters now. They ate only bread and
vegetables—when they could, that is—for you see, they
were very, very poor and ate only once or twice a week.
One day the wife went to the cupboard. . . . (*Curtain*)

*   *   *

Scene Two

TIME: *Long ago.*

SETTING: *The interior of a poor cottage in Norway. There is
an empty table center stage. There is an open window in
the backdrop, and a shelf painted on backdrop, with nothing on it but an empty breadbox.*

AT RISE: MARTHA *and* OLIVER *are onstage.*

MARTHA: Oh, my poor, dear husband. What are we to do?
The cupboard is bare and Christmas is only two days off.

OLIVER: Now, Martha, don't worry that pretty head of

yours. We'll manage somehow. We always have. Remember last year? We had nothing in the cupboard and brother Mervin gave us a box of crackers.

MARTHA: Yes. We are so fortunate that you have such a rich and generous brother. But we just couldn't impose on him again. It wouldn't be right. We musn't take advantage of his wealth and position.

OLIVER: Yes. It would be greedy and unfair—but perhaps I could ask for just a loan. And promise him to return his crackers before the year is over.

MARTHA: That sounds reasonable. He shouldn't miss a box of crackers for a week or two. Why, with all that food he keeps stored in his larder, he could feed the entire army of the kingdom.

OLIVER: Well, a thrifty businessman like my brother deserves to have lots of food and belongings.

MARTHA: Oh, my, yes. I wasn't criticizing him. Why, what would we do with all that food, anyway? It would just spoil on our shelf.

OLIVER: Or make us fat and lazy.

MARTHA: Or give us gout and indigestion.

OLIVER: Or tummy aches.

MARTHA: Yes. . . .

OLIVER *and* MARTHA (*Sighing wistfully*): Ah-h-h!

OLIVER: I'm afraid all this talk of food has made my mouth water.

MARTHA: That's all right, dear. I'll mop up the floor.

OLIVER: And I shall go this very evening to see my brother and ask him to lend us those crackers.

MARTHA: Dress warmly, dear. Be sure to button up your coat.

OLIVER: But, Martha—I have no coat! I sold it last month to the peddler to buy you a broom.

MARTHA: Oh, dear. And I sold the broom to buy you to-
bacco for your pipe.
OLIVER: But, Martha. I sold the pipe. . . .
MARTHA: It's best you go now, dear.
OLIVER: 'Bye, Martha.
MARTHA: 'Bye, Oliver. (*He exits. Curtain.*)

*   *   *

Scene Three

SETTING: *Outside Mervin's mansion. A corner of the mansion, with a working door, is at one side of stage. There is
a tree at opposite side of stage. This scene may be played
before the curtain.*
AT RISE: OLIVER *is talking to* MERVIN *outside the door.*
OLIVER *holds box.*

OLIVER: Thank you, Mervin. You are most generous. After
all, half a box of crackers—even soggy crackers—is better
than none at all. And I shall repay you as soon as possible.
MERVIN: Yes, yes. Now be off. You're letting in some cold
air. And I may have to throw another log on my fire.
OLIVER: Oh! I didn't mean to keep you standing at your
door. And I don't blame you for not letting me in. After
all, my feet are soaking wet and I would have tracked
water all over your beautiful marble floors.
MERVIN: *Humph!* (*He goes inside mansion and slams door.*)
OLIVER: Goodbye, brother dear. (*He turns away.*) How
lucky I am to have such a kind and wealthy brother! I
wish I could visit with him more often, but I know he
has many things to do. He counts his money daily—and
keeps a running inventory of all his riches. It must be ter-

rible to have such wealth and responsibility. I am glad I am not so rich. Why, what would I do with all that gold and all that food? Hmm? Those crackers did look good. Maybe if I had just one. . . . (*Strongly*) No! Martha must have the first one. How selfish of me to think of myself. (DWARF *steps out from behind tree.*)

DWARF: Crackers? Did I hear someone say crackers? Why, they are my favorite dish! I must have them. Please let me have them! Oh, how I love soggy crackers!

OLIVER: Bless me. What a strange little man! (*To* DWARF) Who are you, sir, to be out on a night like this?

DWARF: I might ask you the same—but I won't. I'm too hungry for those crackers you have there. What will you trade for them?

OLIVER: Why, if you are hungry, I will *give* them to you—all but one. Of course I must save that for Martha.

DWARF: Sorry. Dwarfs never take something for nothing. How about trading for this magic mill? (*He takes a small mill out from behind tree.*)

OLIVER: Well, I know nothing of magic. But if it will please you and ease your hunger. . . . (*He holds out box of crackers.*)

DWARF: Good! (*Taking box*) I'll take these crackers—all but one. (*He eats hungrily.*) Yum, yum! (*He presents the mill and cracker box to* OLIVER, *and recites.*)

> Here's a magic mill for you.
> 'Twill make your wishes all come true.
> Whatever you want it grinds with ease.
> All you have to say is "please."
> When the mill has ground enough,
> Just say "thank you" for the stuff.
> And should it fall in greedy hands,
> It will return unto the lands.

Those are the magic words to operate the mill. Remember, "please" and "thank you." No other words will do. (DWARF *disappears*.)

OLIVER: My goodness! He's disappeared! I must hurry home and show Martha. She will like this little mill. It will go nicely with the empty breadbox on the shelf. And she'll have her cracker for Christmas, too! (*Curtain*)

*   *   *

Scene Four

SETTING: *The same as Scene 2.*
AT RISE: MARTHA *and* OLIVER *are talking.*

MARTHA: Oh, Oliver. Did you see the smiles on those poor little orphans' faces when we took them all that food and clothing this afternoon?

OLIVER: Yes—thanks to our little mill. (OLIVER *places mill onstage.*) And now we shall have more than enough crackers to pay back Mervin. I do hope he received the invitation we sent for dinner tonight. It was the least we could do to pay him back.

MARTHA: Oh, I don't blame him if he doesn't come. This place is so small and cold. And his home is so large and warm. But what would we do with all those rooms and servants? They would just get in our way.

OLIVER: Why don't we ask the mill to churn us out a delicious turkey dinner? If Mervin doesn't come, we can give it to our kind neighbors. (MERVIN *appears at window, unnoticed by* MARTHA *and* OLIVER.)

MARTHA: Good idea. And how about a nice, clean tablecloth, too, for Mervin?

OLIVER: Very well. (*Addresses mill*) Magic mill, please turn out a turkey dinner on a nice, clean tablecloth. (*Table top flips over to reveal turkey dinner on white tablecloth. There is a knock on the door.*) Thank you, mill. Perhaps that's Mervin, now. (*He opens the door.*) Oh, dear brother. You did come! (MERVIN *enters.*)

MERVIN: What is this I see? You ask me for crackers one day and the next you have a table laden with goodies.

OLIVER: Oh, brother, you wouldn't believe our good fortune! I have here a magic mill which can grind out our every wish. You need only ask the mill for something and it will immediately fulfill your wish.

MERVIN: Humph! Poppycock! I don't believe it. You probably stole that turkey and are making up that story about the mill.

MARTHA: No, no! It's really true, as you will see. Just name something you like very much and we shall ask the mill to grind it out for you.

MERVIN: Something I like, huh? Let me think! Well . . . I do like hard-boiled eggs. So how about some hard-boiled eggs?

OLIVER: Oh, that should be easy enough. (*To mill*) Magic mill—please grind out some hard-boiled eggs for brother Mervin. (*Mill begins to grind out eggs.* NOTE: *There is a disc inside mill with eggs painted on it, which is slowly turned from backstage, to give illusion that mill is grinding out eggs. See Production Notes.*)

MERVIN: Well—you weren't lying, after all. It *is* a magic mill. (*Mill continues to grind out eggs.*)

MARTHA (*To* OLIVER): Don't you think we should stop it now, Oliver? There must be at least two dozen eggs there. (*There is a knock on the door.*)

OLIVER: Now, who could that be, knocking at our door?

(*He goes to door, opens it.*) Why, it's little Tiny Tim, Bob Cratchit's boy from down the street. Here. . . . (OLIVER *goes back to the table, picks up the turkey and carries it to the door.*) Take this turkey, son. I can always get another one. (*He hands turkey out door, closes door, and returns to center.*)

MERVIN: What? Are you out of your mind? Giving up a perfectly good turkey? (MERVIN *races out door after turkey.*)

OLIVER: We can always get another where that came from. (*Sees mill still grinding eggs*) Oh, my goodness! The magic mill! (*He runs to mill.*) What were the magic words? Oh, yes. (*To mill*) Thank you for the hard-boiled eggs. (*Mill stops grinding eggs and* MERVIN *re-enters carrying turkey.*)

MERVIN: You obviously haven't priced turkey lately. I made that ragamuffin give it back. Oh! You stopped the mill. Good.

MARTHA: Shall we sit down to dinner now?

MERVIN (*Craftily*): I don't see any cranberries on the table.

OLIVER: Oh, I'll ask the magic mill.

MERVIN: No, no. You can't waste the mill's magic on such a trifle. (*Holds out hand*) Here's a nickel. You run down to the store and buy some cranberries.

OLIVER: But, Mervin, it's a five-mile walk to the store.

MERVIN: And Martha, you go with him to make sure he picks out the right kind.

MARTHA: But Mervin, the turkey will get cold.

MERVIN: Never mind. I'll put it back in the oven. Now run along.

OLIVER: Come along, Martha. Mervin's right. Turkey dinner wouldn't be right without cranberry sauce.

MARTHA: You're right, Oliver. Goodbye, Mervin. We will see you in about three or four hours.

MERVIN: Yes, yes. Run along. (*They exit.*) Ha ha! They are gone at last. (*Picks up mill*) I'll just take this mill. Now I shall have everything my greedy heart desires. (*He laughs again and exits. Curtain.*)

*   *   *

Scene Five

TIME: *A few days later.*

SETTING: *On the sea. This scene may be played on top of the puppet stage. A cutout of Mervin's ship is at center, with a cutout of the magic mill on the deck.*

AT RISE: MERVIN *is on board the ship with the* DWARF, *disguised as a sailor.*

MERVIN: Ah—at last! I'm on board my ship—a merchant vessel. And now I'll start making this stupid mill work for me.

DWARF: How will you make money from the mill?

MERVIN: Sailor, I've found out that at the next port the people are badly in need of salt. I'll sell it to them.

DWARF: But those townspeople are poor.

MERVIN: They need salt and I'll make them pay heavily for it. Now, how do you make this mill work? (*To mill*) Mill! Grind salt! (*Nothing happens.*) Grind salt, I tell you! (*Still nothing happens.*) It's not working!

DWARF: Maybe it needs the magic words.

MERVIN: Stay out of this, if you please. (*To mill*) Grind salt! (*It begins grinding salt in great quantities.* NOTE: *A triangle of shiny white fabric is attached behind ship cutout, and the point of the triangle is slowly pulled up by a thread to look as if it is salt filling the ship.*) Look! The mill is doing it! Look at all the beautiful salt! Wonderful, wonderful!

DWARF (*To audience*): It's best I go now. I think he will learn his lesson. (DWARF *disappears.*)

MERVIN: Why, where did that sailor go? Oh, well—never mind. I'll be extra rich when I get into port with all this salt. Grind away, mill! Ha ha! A whole ship full of money-making salt. (*Salt continues to rise in the ship.*) Oh-oh! The boat is beginning to list. Guess that's enough salt. Magic mill—stop grinding salt. (*Salt continues to rise.*) Stop, I say! Stop! (*It continues.*) Oh—the ship is beginning to sink! Help! (*He tries to throw salt over side of ship, to no avail.*) Help! (*The ship sinks out of view of the audience. Curtain.*)

*   *   *

Scene Six

SETTING: *The ocean floor, as in Scene 1. This scene is played behind a sea scrim.*

AT RISE: MERVIN's *ship is seen slowly sinking into the depths of the sea. It settles on the bottom.* GRANNY *and* GILLIE *swim in, in front of the scrim.*

GRANNY: And so, Gillie, the ship sank and the magic mill continued grinding out salt, and so far as anyone knows, it still grinds out salt to this day.

GILLIE: Gee, Grannie, wouldn't it be exciting if someone could find that ship and stop the mill?

GRANNY: That's very unlikely, Gillie. There must be a

million ships at the bottom of the sea. Come. Let's swim to dinner now. No one could possibly find that old ship. (*They swim off, then re-enter behind scrim, and swim across stage, passing ship. A puff of salt emerges from ship as curtain closes.*)

THE END

Production Notes

WHY THE SEA IS SALT

Number of Puppets: 9 hand puppets.

Playing Time: 15 minutes.

Description of Puppets: Granny and Gillie are "moving mouth" or sock hand puppets. Sharkie, Flipper and Charlie are stick puppets, made of paper on heavy wire. Oliver, Martha and Mervin are hand puppets in Norwegian costume. The Dwarf has a long white beard, a stocking cap, and tattered clothes. In Scene 5, the Dwarf wears a sailor's cap.

Properties: Box of "crackers"; model of turkey on heavy wire or dowel; "magic mill," a small coffee grinder, or a box with a revolving handle on the top. There is a window in front of the mill, and a black circular disk with eggs painted on it inside the mill. Turn the disk from behind the mill to give the effect of the mill grinding out hard-boiled eggs.

Setting: Scenes 1 and 6, the ocean floor. A sea scrim or curtain of blue netting with seaweed shapes sewed to it is dropped over the stage. Scenes 2 and 4, Martha and Oliver's poor cottage in Norway. There is a table at center stage. Tabletop is made to flip over; in Scene 2, the bare side of table top is shown, and in Scene 4, the table top turns over and reveals dishes and tablecloth which have been glued on. The turkey is also attached to table but can be removed and held by dowel or wire, so Oliver can pick it up and take it outside. The backdrop has a window cut into it, and painted on the backdrop is a shelf holding an empty breadbox. Scene 3: Outside Mervin's mansion. At one side of stage there is a corner of the mansion, with a working door in it. At the opposite side of stage there is a cut-out of a tree. This scene may be played before the curtain. Scene 5: On the sea. This scene may be played on top of the puppet stage, with the sea scrim in place, with the curtains closed. Then when the ship sinks, open the curtains, and lower ship into the viewing area of the stage for the last scene. The ship is a cardboard cut-out with a cloth sail on a dowel. Put a handle on the back of the ship so that you can hold it easily. Attach a cut-out of the magic mill to the ship. Attach a triangle of shiny white fabric to the back of the ship cut-out, with a thread at the top of the triangle, so that the fabric can be pulled up from behind the ship slowly, to give the effect that salt is rising in the ship.

Lighting: No special effects.

THE PRINCESS AND THE PEA

Adapted from a story by Hans Christian Andersen

Characters

JESTER
PRINCE JACQUES
QUEEN CROWSILDA
GENEVIEVE
HEPZIBAH, *the cat*

Scene One

SETTING: *The hall of the castle. There is a large door center
stage.*
AT RISE: JESTER *is singing and dancing while* PRINCE
JACQUES *watches.*

JESTER (*Singing to the tune of "London Bridge"*):
        To dance a jig and twirl a stick,
        That's the life, just for me.
        You must catch a pretty girl—
        A special princess.

        Time our Jacques gets married, too,
        Takes the throne, starts to rule,
        But the Queen has other plans—
        I'm no fool.

51

(*Speaking*) Come on, Prince Jacques. Cheer up. Things can't be that bad.

JACQUES: Oh, you just don't know. We've had princesses from thirty-five countries or more. Kings, sultans and czars have sent their daughters to be interviewed, but Mother turns them all away. There have been blondes, brunettes, redheads, even bald ones—those didn't appeal to me—but she still says no.

JESTER: That's right—fat ones, skinny ones, some just right —hm-m-m! But Queen Crowsilda just poo-poos them all.

JACQUES: Gosh! That princess yesterday was beautiful.

JESTER: Yes, but she couldn't spin straw into gold.

JACQUES: That did seem an unreasonable requirement on Mother's part. But remember the blonde princess from the day before?

JESTER: The Queen didn't like her name.

JACQUES: Rapunzel, wasn't it? She kept tripping on her braids. A bit clumsy but a lovely girl.

JESTER: And remember the girl who limped? She was pretty. What was wrong with her?

JACQUES: It was the fact that she had only one glass slipper. Mother had a fit because she scratched the castle floors with it. Mama's so fussy.

CROWSILDA (*From offstage; shouting*): Jacques! Jacques!

JESTER: Here comes Queen Crowsilda now. I just remembered. I've got to write a new set of questions for the Queen's quizzes. (*He exits.*)

JACQUES (*Calling after him*): Don't make them too hard! (*To himself*) How can I convince Mama how important it is to have a little princess by my side? (QUEEN CROWSILDA *enters, with* HEPZIBAH, *the cat.*) Good evening, Mama!

CROWSILDA: Oh, there you are, Jacques. It's a wretched evening. It's just pouring rain. (*To cat*) Come, Hepzibah. Stay close to Mama. (*To* PRINCE) I'm simply exhausted from interviewing all those ugly, vulgar girls today.

JACQUES: Oh no, Mama. They were beautiful. I especially liked—

CROWSILDA: She was terrible! All wrong for you. I think we should take a short vacation from all this nonsense and put off the interviews for a while. Perhaps a year or two. I'm afraid none of the princesses will take your mama's place.

JACQUES: But, Mama, I need a princess now! Maybe there will be one more tonight who—

CROWSILDA: Don't be silly. It's raining cats and dogs. No girl in her right mind would come here on a night like this. (*There is a loud knocking at door.*)

JACQUES: Do you hear someone knocking?

CROWSILDA: No!

JACQUES: So do I! I'll show her in. (*He goes out door center.*)

CROWSILDA: Jacques! Come back here! Oh, another of those stupid wretches. I don't know why he insists on marrying. Haven't I been a good mother? I give him all my time. I wear my voice to a frazzle talking to him to keep him company. (GENEVIEVE *enters, center. She is soaking wet.*)

GENEVIEVE: Good evening, Queen Crowsilda. (*She yawns as she curtsies, then shakes out her hair.*)

CROWSILDA: Get away, you soggy ragamuffin! You'll get my beautiful gown all wet.

GENEVIEVE: Oh, excuse me, my lady. It's so late. I've been traveling by coach all night—the rain washed the road away and I had to walk the last mile to your castle. I'm so tired. (*Yawns*)

CROWSILDA: Drippy one, what did you come for?

GENEVIEVE: My father has sent me to be interviewed to marry the Prince.

CROWSILDA: Marry my son?

GENEVIEVE: Yes. I'm a real princess. My hair doesn't look so pretty now, but it's naturally curly.

CROWSILDA: Well, Goldilocks, we will see in the morning.

GENEVIEVE: Not Goldilocks—Genevieve! (*Yawns*)

CROWSILDA: My name is Queen Crowsilda and this is my beautiful cat, Hepzibah.

GENEVIEVE: My name is . . . (*Snores*) Zzz-z-z. (*She falls asleep standing up.* QUEEN *shakes her.*) Yes?

CROWSILDA: Enough talk for tonight. There will be a guest room prepared for you. Kindly dry yourself off. You are making a puddle on my floor.

GENEVIEVE: Thank you, ma'am. I am tired. (*She exits.*)

CROWSILDA: What a wretch she is! My son would never consider marrying such a skinny little water rat.

JACQUES (*Running in*): Mama! Mama! Did you see her? Did you test her? Isn't she great, Mama? She's the one, Mama!

CROWSILDA: It's much too late for interviews or contests tonight. Tomorrow is time enough. I'll test her tomorrow. Now, good night!

JACQUES: I sure liked her looks.

CROWSILDA: I said, *good night!* (*He exits.*) He liked her. *He liked her!* Well, we shall see if she is a real princess or not. (*Calls*) Jester!

JESTER (*Entering*): Yes, Queen Crowsilda?

CROWSILDA: We have one more contestant tonight who thinks she is good enough for my boy. Arrange a bed for her.

JESTER: How will you test her? Should I write more questions and answers for her?

CROWSILDA: No—I've a better idea. We must prove she isn't a real princess. We'll see how sensitive she is. Place one lemon under her mattress tonight.

JESTER: Perhaps a grapefruit would be more fair.

CROWSILDA: Who said anything about being fair? No—on second thought, a pea! And instead of one mattress, make it two—no, ten—no—*twenty mattresses!* Yes. That will do just fine.

JESTER: Anything else, ma'am?

CROWSILDA: I think that will do for now.

JESTER: Yes, ma'am. (*He exits.*)

CROWSILDA: If she is a true princess, she will not sleep a wink and will be bruised from head to toe from that pea. A true princess? Ha! Jacques will just have to wait. Come along, Hepzibah. (*She exits with* HEPZIBAH. *Curtain.*)

* * *

Scene Two

SETTING: *A castle bedroom. There is a low bed at center, with curtains around it.*

AT RISE: GENEVIEVE *enters and heads directly for the bed.*

GENEVIEVE: Oh, boy! Does that bed look comfortable! I'm so tired. (*She falls on bed and immediately begins to snore.*) Zz-z-z-z-z.

CROWSILDA (*Entering with* HEPZIBAH): Genevieve! Oh, dear, she's asleep already. This will never do. (*She leans directly over* GENEVIEVE *and screams*) Wake up!

GENEVIEVE (*Jumping out of bed*): What's wrong? Is the castle on fire?

CROWSILDA: No—it's just that you haven't brushed your hair. True princesses always brush their hair at least 100 strokes before going to bed. (*Inspects her hair*) You had better make it 200. (*Aside*) That should be time enough.

GENEVIEVE (*Yawning*): Yes, ma'am. (*She exits.*)

CROWSILDA (*Calling*): Jester! Jester!

JESTER (*Entering; sleepily*): Yes, ma'am?

CROWSILDA: Have you the mattresses?

√ JESTER: I've only found seventeen of them. Is that enough?

√CROWSILDA: We'll close the bed curtains. You put them on and then we'll see. (*She closes bed curtains.* JESTER *goes inside and mattresses are put on bed.*) Have you got them on yet? (JESTER *comes out from behind bed curtains.*)

√ JESTER: All ready, ma'am.

' CROWSILDA: Let me see! (*She peeks into curtains.*) No, no! Not enough! Go and get your mattress and put it on top.

JESTER: Yes, ma'am. (*He exits.*)

CROWSILDA: We must stop this wretch from marrying my beautiful boy.

JESTER (*Re-entering with mattress*): Here's my mattress.

CROWSILDA: Just put it on top of the others. (*He puts mattress inside bed curtains, comes out, and* CROWSILDA *peeks in again.*) Oh, that is still not high enough. Go and get my mattress. I couldn't sleep tonight, anyway.

JESTER: Yes, ma'am. (*He exits.*)

GENEVIEVE (*From offstage*): I've brushed my hair 200 times. Is that enough?

CROWSILDA: We're not finished—er—you'd better give it another hundred strokes.

GENEVIEVE (*From offstage*): Yes, ma'am.

JESTER (*Re-entering with mattress*): Here's your mattress.

CROWSILDA: Good—good—on top! (*He puts mattress inside bed curtains, comes out, and she looks in again.*) That still isn't quite right. Now, where can we get the twentieth and last one? (*She strokes* HEPZIBAH) Ah, Hepzibah. I'm afraid you will have to sleep on the floor tonight. Jester! Go and get Hepzibah's mattress. That should do it.

JESTER: Yes, ma'am. (*He exits.*)

GENEVIEVE (*From offstage*): Queen Crowsilda! I've brushed my hair three hundred times and it's beginning to fall out.

CROWSILDA: A few more strokes.

GENEVIEVE (*From offstage*): Yes, ma'am.

JESTER (*Entering with mattress*): Here's the cat's bed.

CROWSILDA: Splendid! The frosting on the cake. (*She laughs evilly. He puts mattress on bed.*) Now, let's see what it looks like. (*She opens bed curtains to reveal twenty mattresses.*) Fine! Now off to bed with you. (JESTER *exits.*)

GENEVIEVE (*From offstage*): Am I done yet?

CROWSILDA: Not quite! A few more strokes. (*To herself*) And now for the pea. Where did I put that *petit pois*? (*Reaches into pocket*) Ah—here it is. Now to slip it under the bottom mattress. (*She does so.*) There! If she's a true princess, she won't be able to sleep a wink.

GENEVIEVE (*From offstage*): Now?

CROWSILDA: Now!

GENEVIEVE (*Entering*): I'm ready for bed. (*She yawns.*)

CROWSILDA: And your bed is ready for you.

GENEVIEVE: But I can't climb up!

CROWSILDA: Nonsense. I'll help you up. Just think! Twenty mattresses so you will sleep tight for your contest tomorrow. (HEPZIBAH *digs at bottom mattress.*) Get away from there, Hepzibah. (*To* GENEVIEVE) Now up you go. That's a good girl. (*She helps* GENEVIEVE *to top.*) Are you comfortable?

GENEVIEVE: I think so. (*She yawns again.*)

CROWSILDA: Good. Come, Hepzibah. Good night, *Princess* Genevieve. (*She laughs.*)
GENEVIEVE: Good night, Queen Crowsilda. (CROWSILDA *exits.* HEPZIBAH *stays behind.*) Hm-m-m. (*She tosses.*) I can't seem to get comfortable. (HEPZIBAH *climbs onto bed.*) Get off, kitty! (*She pushes* HEPZIBAH *off bed.*) There must be a soft place somewhere. I'm such a sensitive princess. (HEPZIBAH *gets onto bed again.*) Cat—please! (*She pushes* HEPZIBAH *off again.*) If only I could get to sleep. (HEPZIBAH *gets on bed again.*) Oh, no! (*Curtain*)

*   *   *

Scene Three

TIME: *Next morning.*
SETTING: *Same as Scene 1.*
AT RISE: JACQUES *is anxiously pacing floor.*

JACQUES: It's almost 6:30 in the morning. The day is half gone already. The sun has been up a good half hour. Where is everybody?
JESTER (*Entering*): Did you call me, Prince Jacques? (*He yawns.*)
JACQUES: Yes. Where is everyone?
JESTER: I don't know. I was up half the night with the Queen.
JACQUES: Were you preparing a new contest for Princess Genevieve for today?
JESTER: I guess the test is over already.
JACQUES: What do you mean?
CROWSILDA (*From offstage*): Jester! Jester!
JESTER: You'll find out. (*He quickly exits.*)

JACQUES: I wonder if that pretty little princess is up yet? Here comes Mother. (CROWSILDA *enters.*) Good morning, Mother.

CROWSILDA (*Pleased with herself*): It *is* a good morning, isn't it?

JACQUES: Has she had her test yet? Is she ready? Is it over?

CROWSILDA: I'm sure she is still asleep.

JACQUES: What kind of a test was it, Mama? Was it the question-and-answer kind?

CROWSILDA: No—nor was it the home economics kind.

JACQUES: Not spinning straw into gold?

CROWSILDA: No, no . . . not that. I decided to do something different. Now, you agree that if a girl were a real princess she wouldn't be able to sleep on any hard objects in her bed.

JACQUES: You mean like a mace or a rolling pin? No—I don't think so, Mama.

CROWSILDA: That's what I figured. So last night, while the dear was brushing her straggly hair, I placed one pea beneath her bottom mattress, and—

JACQUES: Bottom mattress?

CROWSILDA: Yes. I put twenty mattresses upon her bed just to insure her comfort.

JACQUES: But she could never feel a pea under twenty—

CROWSILDA: Hush, Jacques. Remember—I am the Queen and I make the rules. She's a true princess *only* if she didn't sleep last night. (*She exits.*)

JACQUES: Not that Mama doesn't want me to marry—but at times I do have my doubts.

GENEVIEVE (*Entering, carrying* HEPZIBAH): Oh, I'm so tired. (*She yawns and drops cat.*)

JACQUES: What's wrong, Princess?

GENEVIEVE: I didn't get a bit of sleep last night. (HEPZIBAH *exits.*) There was something so very hard and uncomfortable in my bed. It must have been a bowling ball. I just couldn't get comfortable.

JACQUES: You didn't sleep at all?

GENEVIEVE: Not at all!

JACQUES: Hooray! You've passed the test. Now we can get married. Hooray! I'm going to run and tell Mama. No—I'll tell the Jester first. Wait here—come with me—no, wait here. I'll be back. I'm so happy. We're going to get married. (*He exits.*)

GENEVIEVE: He seemed a bit anxious, didn't he? (HEPZIBAH *enters, dragging her mattress across stage.*) Oh—there's that cat again.

CROWSILDA (*From offstage; shouting*): Didn't sleep?

GENEVIEVE: Oh-oh! Queen Crowsilda sounds angry.

CROWSILDA (*Entering*): What is this I hear? You didn't sleep at all last night? After I gave you that warm milk, heated the room and arranged all those mattresses to insure your comfort? Of all the ungrateful—

GENEVIEVE (*Falling asleep on her feet again*): Zzz-z-z-z.

CROWSILDA: Well! (*She exits.*)

JESTER (*Running in with* HEPZIBAH, *who is coughing*): Princess, did you see the Queen? Hepzibah has swallowed something and is choking.

GENEVIEVE: Here. Give her to me. I'll fix her. (*She shakes* HEPZIBAH.)

JESTER: Do you think that will do it? (*She shakes* HEPZIBAH *some more.*)

GENEVIEVE: It'll either kill or cure her, in any case. (*She stops shaking cat. It lies panting.*)

JESTER (*Looking closely at cat*): Hepzibah's all right. You saved her.

GENEVIEVE: But, look. (*Points*) There on the floor. She was choking on a small pea. Now, where do you think she could have found that? (JESTER *takes* HEPZIBAH *and exits.*)

JACQUES (*Entering*): There you are, Princess.

GENEVIEVE: Can we live happily ever after now?

JACQUES: Yes, by all means, my little winner—my Princess! (*Curtain*)

THE END

Production Notes

THE PRINCESS AND THE PEA

Number of Puppets: 5 puppets; Hepzibah, the cat, is a non-speaking part.

Playing Time: 15 minutes.

Description of Puppets: French Renaissance dress, or traditional fairy tale costumes for puppets. The Princess wears a simple, long dress, and has a freckled face. When she enters first, she wears a cape and hood of shiny, wet-looking material, to look as if she just came in from the rain. Her hair is made of rayon fringe to move as if it were straight and wet. Queen can be fat or thin, but she must look vain and possessive. Hepzibah is a silly-looking, crosseyed alley cat who seems very much like its mistress—the Queen. Jacques is a simple prince with quizzical brows. The Jester has a resigned expression—he follows the Queen's orders even though he doesn't like to. He wears traditional jester's costume.

Properties: A mattress unit, which is really the fronts of twenty mattresses, sewed together; Jester's mattress, with harlequin design; Queen's mattress, gold; Hepzibah's mattress, very small; a pea.

Setting: Scenes 1 and 3, the hall of the castle, need only a large double door center stage, with a few banners or drapes on walls. Scene 2, the princess's bedroom, consists of a large four-poster bed center stage with draw curtains around it. If you use hand puppets, design the bed with an opening in the bottom in which to put your arm. When the bed curtains are closed, put the mattress unit on the bed from behind, leaving the arm opening so that the Princess can lie on top of the mattresses. If your stage is designed with an open apron in front of the curtain, you can simply close the stage curtains and play in front of them while mattresses are being put on bed. If you are using marionettes, be sure your bed curtain is open on one side for the marionette to get on the bed. Mattresses Jester carries are props not actually put on the bed.

Lighting: No special effects.

SNOW WHITE AND THE SEVEN DWARFS

Adapted from Grimm's fairy tales

Characters

SNOW WHITE
QUEEN
PRINCE CHARMING
HUNTSMAN
MEANIE ⎫
MINEY ⎪
MOE ⎪
DEANIE ⎬ *The Seven Dwarfs*
DINEY ⎪
DOE ⎪
DUM DUM ⎭
RABBIT
DEER
VOICE OF MIRROR

Scene One

TIME: *Long ago.*
SETTING: *The throne room of the Queen's palace. There is a mirror on the wall, and a throne at one side.*
AT RISE: SNOW WHITE *is scrubbing the floor, with a rag and bucket, and singing.*

SNOW WHITE (*Singing to tune of "Twinkle, Twinkle, Little Star"*):

Such a day to wash and dust.
Please the Queen or else she'll bust.
Go outside and wash the stairs,
Stir the soup and mend the tears,
Hope it's time that she does say
I can go outside and play.

(*Speaks*) I've worked since sun-up. My stepmother the Queen does like a clean castle! I wish I had someone to help me clean all these rooms, though. I never worked so hard when Papa was alive. . . . Not that I object to work, but I seldom get to play. (QUEEN *enters.*)

QUEEN: Play, indeed! You are too old to play, and too ugly to let out of the castle. Snow White! My bed hasn't been made yet. Go to my room immediately and change the sheets and air the royal bedroom!

SNOW WHITE: Yes, Stepmother. (*She starts to go.*)

QUEEN: Don't call me Stepmother—I'm your queen. Go now and get busy. There's no time for play. (SNOW WHITE *exits. Mockingly*) "Skin as white as snow—cheeks as red as blood—hair as black as ebony." Ha! Snow White looks more like a skinny kitchen maid to me. Her mother—the first Queen—probably died of disappointment. Now I am Queen and easily the fairest in the land—or so my magic mirror says. But I'll ask it again today, just to be sure. (*She goes to mirror.*)

Mirror, mirror, on the wall
Who's the fairest one of all?

VOICE OF MIRROR:

Yesterday you were the fairest, O Queen,
But today, fairer than Snow White is nowhere seen.

QUEEN: You lie! How dare you! I'm furious! Well—we'll just see who the fairest is tomorrow. (*Calls*) Huntsman! Huntsman! (HUNTSMAN *enters.*)

HUNTSMAN: Yes, my Queen?

QUEEN: I've a small chore for you to do.

HUNTSMAN: Small or large, your wish is my command.

QUEEN: Take Snow White into the woods for a little outing, so she can play. Then when she is not looking—*kill her!*

HUNTSMAN: Oh, no! Sweet innocent Snow White! No! I beg of you—

QUEEN: If you wish to see your family again you *must* do as I say.

HUNTSMAN: I—I. . . .

QUEEN (*Calling*): Snow White! (SNOW WHITE *enters.*)

SNOW WHITE: Yes, Stepmother?

QUEEN: I've changed my mind. You may go out and play in the woods today. The Huntsman will go with you to protect you from harm.

SNOW WHITE: No animal would hurt me. They are all my friends.

QUEEN: Nevertheless, he shall accompany you.

HUNTSMAN: My queen, I—

QUEEN: How were your wife and your *dear* children when you left them this morning?

HUNTSMAN (*Glumly*): I'll take the fair princess to the woods.

QUEEN: Good! Goodbye, *sweet* Snow White. May you have a happy time.

SNOW WHITE: Goodbye—and thank you. (HUNTSMAN *and* SNOW WHITE *exit.*)

QUEEN: Now, magic mirror, we shall see who is the fairest in the land. (*She laughs. Curtain.*)

*　　　*　　　*

Scene Two

SETTING: *In the woods.*

AT RISE: RABBIT *hops across stage.* SNOW WHITE *and* HUNTSMAN *enter. He has a dagger in his hand.*

SNOW WHITE: Come along, good Huntsman. Don't dawdle. It's such a sunny warm day. All my little bird friends are singing to me and there's a little rabbit. I feel so good, not having to stay in that stuffy castle. Thank you for taking me out into the woods today.

HUNTSMAN: Have you no fear, my Snow White, for anything?

SNOW WHITE: Who would want to harm me, good Huntsman? (RABBIT *runs up to her.*) Oh, little rabbit. How sweet you are. Come! Let me pet you. Dear, sweet bunny. (*She pets* RABBIT.)

HUNTSMAN (*Lifting his dagger behind her*): I . . . my family . . . I must— (SNOW WHITE *turns and sees him.*)

SNOW WHITE: Oh! (RABBIT *runs away.*)

HUNTSMAN: I cannot. I can't hurt you, dear princess. (*He kneels.*)

SNOW WHITE: But tell me why you meant me harm!

HUNTSMAN: The Queen means to have you dead. I cannot harm my sweet Snow White.

SNOW WHITE: The Queen? But why?

HUNTSMAN: The magic mirror said that you were the fairest, and the Queen is so vain she wants no one to be more beautiful than she. The Queen must not find out. Run into the woods and do not return . . . or you shall die. Run, Snow White—*run!*

SNOW WHITE: Oh, no! What shall I do? What shall I do? Where can I go?

HUNTSMAN: Goodbye, sweet Snow White. May heaven protect you. (*He exits.*)

SNOW WHITE: Oh, where can I go? Who can help me? What shall I do? (*She begins to cry.* RABBIT *and* DEER *come in and nuzzle* SNOW WHITE. *She cries out in surprise.*) Oh! Oh, it's just a little deer. Hello, little one. Can you help me? Where can I go? (DEER *nudges her.*) Do you know a place? Please lead on. I will follow. (DEER *and* RABBIT *exit, followed by* SNOW WHITE. *Curtain.*)

*　　*　　*

Scene Three

SETTING: *Inside the Dwarfs' cottage. A window overlooking the woods is in the rear wall. At center, there is a table set for seven, with seven little chairs arranged around it.*

AT RISE: SNOW WHITE *enters, followed by* DEER *and* RABBIT.

SNOW WHITE: I wonder who lives here? Sweet little rabbit and deer, won't you stay? (*They exit.*) Don't run away! Oh, well—never mind. Perhaps they will come back. (*She looks around.*) Such a funny little house. There must be (*Counts dishes*)—one, two, three, four, five, six—seven little children living here. They certainly are tidy. Everything is so neat! The table is all set for dinner. Seven little loaves of bread with seven little glasses of wine. *Wine?* For children? (*Shakes head*) I'll just take a bite from one of the loaves of bread. (*She does.*) Mm-m-m. That's good. I wonder if they would allow me to stay here for a little while? I'm so tired. I'll just lie down for a moment until they get home. (*Yawns*) I wonder where they could be? (*Yawns again*) Seven little children! And no mommy. (*Goes to side of stage*) Here is the bedroom. (*She exits.*)

DWARFS (*Singing from offstage to the tune of "London Bridge Is Falling Down"*):

>Home we go from copper mine!
>Hard day's work—suits us fine.
>Seven dwarfs, not eight or nine—
>Hungry and tired.

MEANIE (*From offstage*): Wait, brothers. The door is open!

MINEY (*From offstage*): Is there a thief inside?

MOE (*Entering*): Come on in, men. We probably just forgot to lock the door and left it open this morning. (*The other Dwarfs—*MEANIE, MINEY, DEANIE, DINEY, DOE *and* DUM DUM—*enter.*)

DEANIE: Time for dinner. Everyone wash up!

DINEY: Bring in the wash tub, Dum Dum. (DUM DUM *goes out.*)

DOE: Am I hungry!

MOE: We all are starved from working all day in the copper mine. We should have enough copper to take to town soon. (DUM DUM *enters with a big wash tub.*)

DUM DUM: Here we are. Everyone clean up. (*Dwarfs crowd around tub.*)

DWARFS (*Singing to tune of "London Bridge"*):

>Scrub away the hard day's grime.
>Dinner's done—just in time.
>Bread and meat and cake and wine—
>Couldn't be better!

(*They all laugh and take the wash tub offstage, then go to table.*)

MEANIE: Ho, brothers! Part of my bread is missing. Someone has eaten it! There are crumbs about.

MINEY: Maybe they are still in the house!

Dum Dum: The bread crumbs?

Miney: No, Dum Dum, the thieves!

Moe: They could be. Search every nook and cranny!

Deanie: I'm scared!

Meanie: Don't be a scaredy cat. You look in the bedroom and—

Snow White (*Yawning loudly, from offstage*): Ah-h-h!

Diney: What was that? (Deanie *exits into bedroom.*)

Miney: It sounds like a ghost. (Deanie *re-enters, running.*)

Deanie: It is a ghost! It's—(*Breaks off as* Snow White *enters*)

Snow White: I slept so soundly. (*She sees Dwarfs.*) Oh! You are not little children at all!

Meanie: No—of course not! We are seven dwarf brothers. (*Pointing*) This is Miney. That is Moe, Deanie, Diney, Doe, and Dum Dum, and I am Meanie.

Dum Dum: Who are you?

Snow White: I am Snow White.

Doe: Princess Snow White?

Snow White: Yes. I had to run away because the Queen wanted me to be killed. I can never return. (*She begins to cry.*)

Dum Dum: Don't cry. You can stay with us.

Meanie: Well—I don't know about—

Others (*Together*): Yes! She stays! She stays!

Diney: We will protect you from the Queen.

Snow White: You are all too kind. Thank you very much. (*Yawns*) But I'm afraid I'm still tired.

Dum Dum: You just go back to the bedroom and sleep. We will sleep out here. And tomorrow we will build you a pretty bed.

Snow White: Oh, thank you. We shall all be so happy here!

Dwarfs (*Singing to tune of "London Bridge"*):

Now we have a lady friend,
Sweet Snow White—we'll defend.
Just our luck the Queen did send
A lovely Princess.
(*Dwarfs dance about* Snow White *as curtain falls.*)

*   *   *

Scene Four

Setting: *The dungeon. The mirror is hanging on the wall. There is a bench at center with bottles and flasks on it.*
At Rise: Queen *rushes in.*

Queen: Mirror, mirror—Princess Snow White is dead. Now who is the fairest one of all? (*Cackles*)
Voice of Mirror:
Fair indeed, are you, O Queen,
But fairer than Snow White is nowhere seen.
Happy she lives, beyond words to tell,
Where the Dwarfs of the Copper Mountain dwell.
Queen: No! It is impossible! The Huntsman killed Snow White in the woods.
Voice of Mirror: Snow White lives with the good Seven Dwarfs this day.
Queen: I'll kill her myself. I will! First I'll drink a magic potion to turn myself into an ugly old woman. What are the magic words? Oh, yes. (*Recites*)
Ugly see and ugly do.
Let me look as few can do,
Just long enough to kill my ward—
That will be my sole reward.
(Queen *takes a bottle from bench and drinks from it.*)

Ah-h-h! (*She falls behind bench, then re-appears as an ugly old woman. She staggers to mirror.*) Mirror, mirror—now how do I look? (*She cackles.*)

VOICE OF MIRROR: Oh, Queen, I—

QUEEN: Never mind. I don't want to hear. I know how I look. But I'll only be this way long enough to kill Snow White. (*Laughs again*) And now for the apple. (*Holds up her hand, revealing bright red apple*) Here we are! A beautiful—red—*poisoned* apple! (*She exits, laughing evilly. Curtain.*)

*　　　*　　　*

Scene Five

SETTING: *Outside the Dwarfs' cottage.*

AT RISE: SNOW WHITE *enters from cottage.*

SNOW WHITE (*Calling*): Hurry, now. It's time for work. (*Dwarfs file out of cottage.*)

MINEY: We're off to work, Snow White.

MOE: You be careful today. If the Queen finds that you are alive, goodness knows what will happen to you.

DEANIE: She will try to kill Snow White!

DWARFS: Ooo!

DINEY: We had better stay at home.

SNOW WHITE: Nonsense! How could she know where I am? Now, off you go.

DUM DUM: Will you be all right?

SNOW WHITE: Yes—of course.

DOE: Don't let anyone in the house, Snow White.

MOE: And don't let anyone give you anything.

SNOW WHITE: I'll be all right. And careful too.

MEANIE: We had better go, men. The copper mine waits without.

SNOW WHITE: Without what?

MINEY: Without us to work in it! (*All laugh.*) Come on, brothers, off we go.

SNOW WHITE: Goodbye for now, boys.

DWARFS: Goodbye, Snow White. (*Dwarfs exit.*)

SNOW WHITE: Such sweet little dwarfs. I think I'm going to like it here. Now to bake them a delicious apple pie. Oh . . . I don't think there are any apples. I'll just go inside and see. (*She exits.* QUEEN *enters, in disguise of an ugly old woman. She carries an apple in her hand, and has a basket of apples over her arm.*)

QUEEN: Apples, indeed! (*She knocks on cottage door.*) Apples! Apples for sale! (*She cackles.*)

SNOW WHITE (*Opening door*): Did you say you had apples for sale?

QUEEN: Yes. Delicious red apples. And so reasonable.

SNOW WHITE: But I'm afraid I don't have any money. Are they good apples?

QUEEN: Good? Of course, my dear. Come—try one! They are so red—and delicious. (*Holds out apple in her hand.*)

SNOW WHITE: They do look good, old lady.

QUEEN: Just try one bite—to see how they taste.

SNOW WHITE: Well—maybe just a bite. (*She bites into apple, and gasps, then falls to ground and lies motionless.*)

QUEEN (*Laughing*): Ha ha! Now, mirror—who is the fairest? Snow White is dead and now I'm the fairest in the land. Well, at least I will be after this potion wears off. It should be gone now . . . now that Snow White is. . . . (*Worried*) Why doesn't the potion wear off? It's time, but—something is wrong! (*Pats her face*) My face! I'm still an ugly old woman. Oh, no! I'm still ugly! What will

I do? The potion has set in for ever. Now I'll never be beautiful again. What can I do? What can I do? Oh, no-o-o! (*She runs offstage. Curtain.*)

*   *   *

Scene Six

SETTING: *A hillside.*
AT RISE: SNOW WHITE *is lying motionless on a bed. Dwarfs are standing around her, crying.*

MOE: She was so beautiful. (*Sobs*)
DEANIE: We don't have the heart to bury her. How could we bury Snow White in the cold, dark ground?
DINEY: We should never have left her side.
DOE: She *is* still beautiful.
MINEY: Just as if she were sleeping.
MEANIE: What will we do without her?
DUM DUM: I miss our Snow White. (*He weeps and they all cry softly.* PRINCE CHARMING *comes in.*)
PRINCE: Dear Seven Dwarfs, who is this beautiful maiden that lies as if dead?
MOE: She is our beloved Snow White. The Queen came in the disguise of an ugly old woman and killed Snow White with a poisoned apple.
MEANIE: But one thing! The Queen cannot rid herself of that ugly face. *Just punishment.* Never again will she be beautiful.
MINEY: Nor will our Snow White. (*Sobs*)
PRINCE: Snow White will always be beautiful. (*He bends and kisses her.*)

SNOW WHITE (*Waking up*): Oh . . . What happened? Who are you?

PRINCE: Your devoted Prince Charming.

SNOW WHITE: And my seven little dwarfs?

PRINCE: Here they are—by your side.

MEANIE: Look, men! Snow White is alive. Our Snow White is alive!

DWARFS (*Ad lib*): Hurray! She's alive—our Snow White is alive! (*Etc.*)

PRINCE: Now, won't you come with me? I've been searching for a wife to complete my life.

MINEY: Go with him, Snow White.

MOE: Be his bride!

DWARFS: And be happy!

SNOW WHITE (*Rising*): Dear, dear little Dwarfs. I shall never forget you.

PRINCE: You must all come to our wedding.

DUM DUM: Will there be bread and wine?

PRINCE: Of course.

DWARFS (*Together*): We'll be there!

SNOW WHITE: Goodbye, my friends.

DWARFS: Goodbye, our dear Snow White. (PRINCE *and* SNOW WHITE *exit. Curtain.*)

THE END

Production Notes

Snow White and the Seven Dwarfs

Number of Puppets: 14 hand puppets (or marionettes), and offstage Voice of Mirror. This show will take lots of puppeteers, so be sure to have a big stage with room for many people backstage.

Playing Time: 15 minutes.

Description of Puppets: The puppets can be designed after the Walt Disney movie, but try to be original and invent new costumes. Snow White is very pretty, with black hair, fair skin, and rosy cheeks. The Queen must be very beautiful, yet stern and vain. She wears lots of jewelry. Make a second puppet for the Queen when she changes herself into an ugly old woman: She should have an ugly face and wear dark clothes, with a shawl over her head. Sew an apple into her hand. The Huntsman is in browns and greens, with a dagger sewn to his hand. The Dwarfs are short, round, and have beards. They wear jackets and stocking caps. Prince Charming is handsome. He wears a cape and hat. If the stage is big enough, he might even ride a horse.

Properties: Wash tub (find one large enough for all the Dwarfs to wash in); bucket and cloth; apple basket.

Setting: Scene 1, the throne room—use a draped background, with a throne at one side (or painted on backdrop), and a mirror on wall. Scene 2, in the woods—a plain background with a few cut-out trees against it. Scene 3, inside the Dwarfs' cottage—a table set for seven, with seven chairs around it, is at center (or may be painted on backdrop). Backdrop also shows window overlooking woods. Scene 4, the dungeon—a dark background, with a workbench full of bottles and flasks at center (or painted on backdrop). Arches or hanging chains may be painted on backdrop. Scene 5, outside the cottage—cottage exterior is painted on backdrop (or else a cut-out of the cottage with an open window and door can be onstage). Scene 6, a hillside—show a flowery hillside and blue sky on the backdrop. There is a simple bed at center, for Snow White.

Lighting: No special effects.

PINOCCHIO

Adapted from a story by Carlo Collodi

Characters

GEPPETTO, *an old wood carver*
PINOCCHIO, *the wooden puppet*
CREEKO THE CRICKET
BEGGAR WOMAN
BLUE FAIRY
BLACKBEARD, *a puppeteer*
PUNCHINELLO ⎫
HARLEQUIN ⎬ *his puppets*
FOX, *a crook*
CAT, *his accomplice*
FALCON
DOGFISH
PINOCCHIO, *the real boy*

Scene One

SETTING: *A sparsely furnished carpenter's shop. There is a window in the back, and a workbench with tools and an upright log on top of it. A couch is on one side.*
AT RISE: CREEKO THE CRICKET *comes in and addresses the audience.*

CREEKO: Once upon a time there was—a king, you exclaim? No, children, you are wrong. Once upon a time there was a piece of wood. It was not valuable. Just a plain stick of wood such as you have seen burned in a stove or fireplace. (GEPPETTO *enters.*) There was also a carpenter named Geppetto who owned this piece of wood. He lived in a little room with his carpentry tools and a few sticks of furniture, for he was very poor. (CREEKO *exits.*)

GEPPETTO: I suppose my friend Master Cherry thought I was crazy to want this wood to make a marionette, but I'm too poor to marry, and I've always wanted a boy of my own. So a puppet it shall be. (GEPPETTO *takes hammer and pounds away at log on table.* NOTE: *Log is really a hollow tube covering* PINOCCHIO. *As* GEPPETTO *hits the tube with his hammer, it slowly is lowered into table, gradually revealing* PINOCCHIO.) First the head. (*Head appears*) Wooden eyes—why do you stare at me? (*More hammering*) And now for the mouth. (*He hammers.* PINOCCHIO *laughs.*) What was that? (*He goes to window.*) Who's laughing at me? (PINOCCHIO *laughs again.* GEPPETTO *turns back to log.*) So it's you! Stop laughing, boy. Now to carve the arms and legs. (*Hammers some more*) Stop wiggling, you young rascal. You are not yet completed and already you are misbehaving. (*He reveals the rest of the puppet.*) And now the legs. . . . There! (PINOCCHIO *kicks him.*) Don't kick me, you bad boy. (PINOCCHIO *laughs.*) You should have a name. Hm-m-m. I'll call you Pinocchio. And now let's put you on the floor and see if you can walk. (*Puts* PINOCCHIO *on floor.*) One step at a time—left. . . . (PINOCCHIO *tries to walk.*) Right. . . . Fine! (PINOCCHIO *runs around room.*) Now you must learn to talk.

PINOCCHIO: Learn to talk? But I know how to talk already, Papa.

GEPPETTO: Amazing! But it will soon be dawn and you will have to go to school. I must buy you a spelling book. I'll be right back. (GEPPETTO *leaves.*)

PINOCCHIO: Ah! He's gone. Now I'll run away. I don't want to go to school.

CREEKO (*Entering*): Cree-cree-crik. . . .

PINOCCHIO: Who's calling me?

CREEKO: I am.

PINOCCHIO: Who are you?

CREEKO: I'm Creeko, the talking cricket. I am your conscience.

PINOCCHIO: Go away at once!

CREEKO: I will not go until I have told you a great truth.

PINOCCHIO: Tell it then, and be quick about it.

CREEKO: Woe to boys who rebel against their parents and run away from home. Sooner or later they will be sorry.

PINOCCHIO: Creeko Cricket, you keep still!

CREEKO: I will see you again, dear Pinocchio. (*He exits.*)

GEPPETTO (*Entering with a spelling book*): It's morning, Pinocchio, and time to go to school.

PINOCCHIO: I'm not dressed properly.

GEPPETTO: But you are clean! Remember that it is not fine clothes, but clean clothes that mark a gentleman.

PINOCCHIO: But to go to school I lack the most important thing.

GEPPETTO: What is that?

PINOCCHIO: A spelling book.

GEPPETTO: Ah, but I have one. I sold my coat to buy your spelling book. Now off to school, my boy. (*He gives book to* PINOCCHIO.)

PINOCCHIO: Goodbye, Papa.

GEPPETTO: Goodbye, Pinocchio. Come straight home for dinner. I'll be waiting for you. (*Curtain*)

*   *   *

Scene Two

SETTING: *A street. This scene may be played in front of the curtain.*

AT RISE: PINOCCHIO *skips onstage.*

PINOCCHIO (*Sing-song*): Off to school I go. Off to school I— (*He finds a penny on the street.*) I've found a penny! Today is my lucky day. Today I will learn to read, tomorrow I will learn to write, and the next day to cipher. Then with all my education I shall earn a great deal of money, and I'll buy my papa a new coat of gold and silver with diamond buttons.

BEGGAR WOMAN (*Entering*): May I have a penny? I'm poor and very hungry.

PINOCCHIO: I need my penny to buy candy at school. Find your own penny. (BEGGAR WOMAN *turns into the* BLUE FAIRY. *See Production Notes.*) Where did the old beggar woman go? And who are you?

BLUE FAIRY: I am the Blue Fairy, your guardian. That old lady was hungry. You had breakfast this morning. You must learn not to be selfish, Pinocchio. When you are selfish and greedy, you are many steps from becoming a real boy. For you to be a real boy would please your papa.

PINOCCHIO: And me, too. I want to be a real boy.

BLUE FAIRY: Then be good, and off to school with you.

PINOCCHIO: Goodbye, fair guardian. (*She exits.*) Off to school I go. (*Faint music is heard from offstage.*) Off to school. . . . (*Music gets louder.*) What can that music be? It's so pretty. (BLACKBEARD *enters, grinding a hand organ, which reads,* GREAT PUPPET THEATER.) Today I will listen to music. Tomorrow I will go to school. (*He goes up to* BLACKBEARD) What does that say on the side of your music box?

BLACKBEARD: It says, Great Puppet Theater!

PINOCCHIO: How much does it cost to get in? I have a penny.

BLACKBEARD: Two pence.

PINOCCHIO: Will you give me two pence for this new spelling book?

BLACKBEARD: I will buy the spelling book for two pence. (*They exchange book and coins.*)

PINOCCHIO: Hooray! I get to see the puppet show today. (*He exits with* BLACKBEARD.)

BLUE FAIRY (*From offstage*): Pinocchio—remember your papa's coat! (*Curtain.*)

*   *   *

Scene Three

SETTING: *Blackbeard's puppet theater. There is a miniature puppet stage at rear.*

AT RISE: HARLEQUIN *and* PUNCHINELLO, BLACKBEARD's *puppets, are dancing on the miniature puppet stage in time to music.* PINOCCHIO *enters and watches them.*

HARLEQUIN (*Stopping his dance and pointing to* PINOCCHIO): Am I awake or dreaming? Surely that's Pinocchio!

PUNCHINELLO: It is indeed Pinocchio.

HARLEQUIN: It is! It is! It's our brother, Pinocchio!

PUNCHINELLO: Long live Pinocchio!

HARLEQUIN: Come up here and greet us, dear friend. (PINOCCHIO *runs up on the puppet stage and embraces them.*)

BLACKBEARD (*From offstage*): Go on with the play, puppets! (BLACKBEARD *comes onstage. To* PINOCCHIO) Why have you come to raise a disturbance in my theater? Come with me. (*He picks up* PINOCCHIO.)

PUNCHINELLO: Oh, poor Pinocchio.

HARLEQUIN: It's our fault.

BLACKBEARD: There is not enough wood for roasting my sheep tonight. Pinocchio is made of very dry wood and will make a beautiful blaze for my roast.

PINOCCHIO: Papa! Papa! Save me! I don't want to die! I don't want to die! (*All three puppets cry.*)

BLACKBEARD (*Sneezing*): Ah-h-h-h-choo! Ah-h-h-h-choo!

HARLEQUIN (*To* PUNCHINELLO): Good news. Blackbeard sneezed. That is a sign that he pities Pinocchio and will spare him.

BLACKBEARD: Ah-h-h-h-choo!

PINOCCHIO (*To* BLACKBEARD): Bless you!

BLACKBEARD: Thank you. Your papa and mama—are they still alive?

PINOCCHIO: Papa, yes. My mama I have never known.

BLACKBEARD: What a sorrow it would have been for the poor man if I had thrown you on the burning coals. Instead, I will burn a puppet belonging to my company. Ah! Which one? I know! (*He grabs* HARLEQUIN.)

HARLEQUIN: No! No! Not me!

PINOCCHIO (*On his knees*): Have pity! Sir Blackbeard!

BLACKBEARD: What do you want of me?

PINOCCHIO: I beg of you to pardon poor Harlequin.

BLACKBEARD: Impossible. I have spared you, so he must be put on the fire—for I am determined to have my mutton well roasted.

PINOCCHIO: Then in that case I know my duty. Throw me

into the flames. It is not just that my true friend Harlequin should die for me. (*All puppets cry.*)

BLACKBEARD: Ah-h-h-choo! Ah-h-h-choo! You are a good brave boy, Pinocchio.

HARLEQUIN: Then I'm free?

BLACKBEARD: You are free. Tonight I will resign myself to eating my mutton half-raw.

PINOCCHIO, HARLEQUIN *and* PUNCHINELLO: Hooray!

BLACKBEARD: What is your Papa's name, Pinocchio?

PINOCCHIO: Geppetto.

BLACKBEARD: Is he poor?

PINOCCHIO: Very poor.

BLACKBEARD: Poor fellow. I'm sorry for him. Here! Take these five gold pieces and give them to him with my compliments. (BLACKBEARD *gives* PINOCCHIO *a bag of gold.*)

PINOCCHIO: I thank you a thousand times. Now I must go home. Goodbye, my friends.

ALL: Goodbye, Pinocchio. (PINOCCHIO *exits. Curtain.*)

*　　　*　　　*

Scene Four

SETTING: *A street, played before the curtain as in Scene 2.*

AT RISE: PINOCCHIO *enters.*

PINOCCHIO: Home I go, to see my papa again! (Fox *and* CAT *enter.* Fox *has a crutch under his arm, and* CAT *wears dark glasses.*)

FOX: Good evening, Pinocchio.

PINOCCHIO: How do you know my name?

Fox: I know your father well. I saw him a while ago, shivering in the doorway of his house, looking for you.

Pinocchio: Poor Papa. But in the future he will not need to shiver.

Cat: Not shiver? Why, Pinocchio?

Pinocchio: Because I have become a gentleman.

Fox *and* Cat (*Laughing*): You?

Pinocchio: There is nothing to laugh at. If you know money when you see it, you will know that these are five gold pieces. (*He shows them the bag of gold.* Fox *lifts his crutch and the* Cat *raises his dark glasses.*)

Fox: Hm-m-m-m. And what are you going to do with all that money?

Pinocchio: I shall buy my papa a new coat, and a spelling book for myself—for I wish to go to school to study.

Fox: Look at me. Through my foolish desire to study I became lame.

Cat: And look at me. Because I was so fond of study I lost the sight of both my eyes.

Pinocchio (*Gullibly*): Really?

Fox: Would you like to double your money? Would you like to turn your five miserable gold pieces into a hundred . . . a thousand . . . two thousand?

Pinocchio: Yes, of course, but how?

Fox: Easy enough. Instead of going home, you must go with us to the field of miracles.

Pinocchio: The field of miracles?

Cat: The field of miracles!

Fox: Come. We will show you the way.

Pinocchio: When I'm rich I'll give each of you 500 gold coins to show my appreciation.

Fox: To us? We do not work for profit. We work only to help others.

CAT: Yes. . . . to help others. (*They all exit together.*)
BLUE FAIRY (*Entering*): Pinocchio! Come back! Your papa is looking for you. (*Curtain.*)

*　　*　　*

Scene Five

SETTING: *The field of miracles. There are a tree and two pails onstage.*
AT RISE: PINOCCHIO *enters with* FOX *and* CAT.

FOX: Ah—here we are, at last.
PINOCCHIO: That was a long walk and I'm tired.
CAT: But it will be worth it to you.
FOX: We will leave you now. Plant your coins right here, under this tree. Pour two buckets of water on them and one pinch of salt. Then leave them for a short while.
CAT: When you return you will have your fortune growing on a tree.
FOX: Goodbye. And remember—plant them *right here!*
PINOCCHIO: Thank you ever so much, friends. (*They exit, leaving* PINOCCHIO.) Now—I'll just drop my five gold coins into this hole, and . . .
CREEKO (*Entering*): Beware, Pinocchio!
PINOCCHIO: Who is it?
CREEKO: It's Creeko, the Cricket, again.
PINOCCHIO: What do you want this time?
CREEKO: Turn back and take the five gold pieces to your poor papa, who is crying because you have not returned to him.
PINOCCHIO: Tomorrow my papa will be a gentleman. By then these five coins will have become five thousand.

CREEKO: Don't trust those who promise to make you rich in a day. Go back.

PINOCCHIO: I don't need your advice. Good night, Creeko Cricket.

CREEKO: Good night, Pinocchio. Heaven keep you from robbers. (CREEKO *exits*.)

PINOCCHIO: And good riddance. And now to plant my gold. (*He drops the bag of gold into a hole under the tree*.) There! And now the two pails of water. (*Pretends to pour water from pails*) And now a pinch of salt. (*Pretends to sprinkle salt*) There! Now I'll walk around this field of miracles and wait for my gold tree to grow. By the time I come back this way it should be fully grown and I'll just pull the gold right off. Papa and I are going to be rich! (PINOCCHIO *exits*. CAT *and* Fox *re-enter and take the bag of gold*.)

Fox: The stupid, wooden-headed fool! (Fox *and* CAT *exit*.)

PINOCCHIO (*Entering*): My tree should be grown by now. I . . . (*Looks for the gold tree*) Perhaps I'm too early . . . or maybe I didn't plant them right. I'll try a different spot. (*He looks for the bag of gold*.) Oh, no! The gold isn't here. What happened?

BLUE FAIRY (*Entering*): What's wrong, Pinocchio? Where is the gold for your papa?

PINOCCHIO: I gave my gold to the poor. (*His nose grows longer*.)

BLUE FAIRY: Now, Pinocchio, look at your nose. You aren't telling me the truth.

PINOCCHIO: Well—I lost the money in the river. (*His nose grows still longer*.)

BLUE FAIRY: Look again. Your nose grows even more.

PINOCCHIO: Oh! I swallowed the gold coins. . . . (*Nose grows even longer*)

BLUE FAIRY: You see—the more you tell lies, the longer your nose grows.

PINOCCHIO: Oh, my beautiful Blue Fairy, the Fox and Cat told me to bury the gold to make more money, and now they are gone—Fox, Cat, and the money.

BLUE FAIRY: You are a very stupid puppet. At this rate you will never be a real boy. But now you must hurry to save your papa. He has gone to sea looking for you and he is in great danger. (*She claps and her* FALCON *enters.*) Get on my falcon's back and fly out to sea to save your father.

PINOCCHIO: Yes, Blue Fairy! Yes! I must save him. Goodbye. (PINOCCHIO *gets on* FALCON's *back and they fly about.*)

BLUE FAIRY: Goodbye, Pinocchio. (*They exit. Curtain.*)

* * *

Scene Six

SETTING: *At sea.*

AT RISE: FALCON, *with* PINOCCHIO *on his back, flies in.*

PINOCCHIO: Where is my papa? (*Calls*) Papa! Papa!

FALCON: Caw! Caw! Out to sea. Caw!

PINOCCHIO: Take me to him. (*Calling*) Papa! Papa! (*They fly about.*) Where's my papa?

FALCON: The gulls say his boat sank and the dogfish swallowed him.

PINOCCHIO: I must help him! (PINOCCHIO *jumps from* FALCON's *back into ocean.* FALCON *flies offstage.*) Papa! Papa! (PINOCCHIO *swims about.* DOGFISH *enters and swallows* PINOCCHIO. *Curtain.*)

* * *

Scene Seven

SETTING: *Inside Dogfish's stomach.*
AT RISE: GEPPETTO *is on one side of the stage.* PINOCCHIO *enters.*

PINOCCHIO: It's so dark in here. I must be in the dogfish's stomach. But, wait—who is that? There is someone else in here with me.

GEPPETTO: It is only Geppetto, once a poor wood carver, but now food for the dogfish.

PINOCCHIO: Papa! My dear papa! I have found you at last. I will never, never leave you again. (*Crosses to* GEPPETTO)

GEPPETTO: Can I believe my eyes? Are you really my boy, Pinocchio?

PINOCCHIO: Yes! Yes! I am really your wooden puppet. Have you forgiven me?

GEPPETTO: Oh, my dear boy! (*They embrace.*)

PINOCCHIO: I've had such a time and have such a tale to tell. But we must escape through the mouth of the dogfish and swim away.

GEPPETTO: But I cannot swim.

PINOCCHIO: I will carry you on my shoulders. I am made of wood and can float. Now, come. The dogfish is asleep with his mouth open. (*They exit through teeth at front. Curtain.*)

*   *   *

Scene Eight

SETTING: *Geppetto's workshop, as in Scene 1.*
AT RISE: GEPPETTO, *sick, is lying on couch.* PINOCCHIO *stands by him.*

PINOCCHIO: Poor Papa. Please get well. I've worked every day since we returned from the sea. I've gone to school, too, and now you must get well. Here are some copper farthings I've earned drawing water for the farmers next door. Get well, Papa.
BLUE FAIRY (*Entering*): Pinocchio!
PINOCCHIO: My Blue Fairy has returned.
BLUE FAIRY: I see that you are a good puppet now. And you have been taking care of your papa. Would you like to be a real boy now?
PINOCCHIO: I would rather see my papa well, Blue Fairy.
GEPPETTO (*Weakly*): Pinocchio. . . .
PINOCCHIO: Yes, Papa?
GEPPETTO: Would you get me a glass of cool water?
PINOCCHIO: Yes, Papa. (PINOCCHIO *exits.*)
BLUE FAIRY: And now it is time for the real boy. Sit up, old Geppetto. (*He sits.*)
GEPPETTO: Suddenly I feel so much better!
BLUE FAIRY: Now, greet your boy, Papa Geppetto.
GEPPETTO: What? Who's there? (PINOCCHIO, *the boy, enters.*)
PINOCCHIO: It's me, Papa! Look at me!
GEPPETTO: My *son!* You're a real boy!
BLUE FAIRY: Well done, Pinocchio. To reward you for your kind heart I will forgive you for all that is past. Try to be good in the future and you will be happy. Goodbye, Pinocchio.

PINOCCHIO: Goodbye, my dear Blue Fairy. And thank you! (*She exits.* PINOCCHIO *and* GEPPETTO *exit in the opposite direction.* CREEKO THE CRICKET *enters.*)

CREEKO (*Calling*): Pinocchio! Pinocchio! Ah . . . I guess he doesn't need a conscience any more. Well. . . . Perhaps there's someone out there who needs me more! (*Peers out into audience, as curtains close.*)

THE END

Production Notes

PINOCCHIO

Number of Puppets: 13 puppets or marionettes. The Beggar Woman may be quickly exchanged for Blue Fairy, or else a turn-around puppet may be made, with Beggar Woman on one side and Blue Fairy on the other.

Playing Time: 15 minutes.

Description of Puppets: Pinocchio is a small puppet, and wears a bright jacket and short pants. Pinocchio's nose should be made so that it pulls out of his head, or else longer noses can be added. Creeko wears a jacket and top hat. Harlequin and Punchinello are small puppets, and they wear white costumes. Harlequin's has diamond-shaped patches. Blackbeard has a long black beard and is very tall. Fox carries a crutch and Cat wears dark glasses. Falcon is a white bird. If a marionette is used, it can be made to fly easily, otherwise a puppet on a long stick can be worked from below. The boy Pinocchio is dressed like the puppet, but is taller.

Properties: Hammer; miniature hand organ, reading GREAT PUPPET THEATER; penny; bag of gold pieces; two pails.

Setting: Scene 1: Geppetto's workshop, with a carpenter's bench, tools and an upright, hollow tube, painted to resemble a log, which conceals Pinocchio. Tube is gradually lowered through hole in carpenter's bench to reveal Pinocchio. There are a window and a couch at rear. Scene 2: A street. This scene may be played before the curtain. Scene 3: The Great Puppet Theater. A miniature puppet stage is at rear. Scene 4: A street. Scene may be played before the curtain. Scene 5: The field of miracles. A tree is at one side, and two pails stand nearby. Scene 6: At sea. A backdrop of the sea, with waves, etc., is used. Scene 7: Inside the Dogfish's stomach. Two rows of jagged teeth are at top and bottom of stage. Red paper may be used as backdrop, lighted from behind. Scene 8: Geppetto's workshop, the same as Scene 1.

Lighting: Special effects in Scene 7, as indicated above.

THE RELUCTANT DRAGON

Adapted from a story by Kenneth Grahame

Characters

ROBERT, *a boy*
ROBERT'S MOTHER
SHEPHERD
DRAGON
MRS. SMYTHE
ST. GEORGE

Scene One

TIME: *Long ago.*
SETTING: *A kitchen interior, in an English cottage.*
AT RISE: ROBERT *is on the floor, reading a large book.*
ROBERT'S MOTHER *is cooking, holding a bowl and spoon.*

MOTHER: Robert! Put your book away now. It's nearly time
for supper.
ROBERT: Just let me finish this one story. It's all about dragons, giants, and dwarfs.
MOTHER: All right, child. (*Thoughtfully*) I've often won-
dered if there really are such things as dragons, giants and
dwarfs.
ROBERT: Oh, there surely are, Mother. It says so in these
wonderful books I've borrowed.
MOTHER: Oh? Perhaps, book learning is useful, in spite of

95

what the neighbors say. (*Sound of pounding on door is heard.*)

SHEPHERD (*From offstage*): It's all up! Help! It's all up for us. Open up! (ROBERT *opens door and* SHEPHERD *runs in.*)

MOTHER: What's wrong, Shepherd?

SHEPHERD: I'll never go up on the Downs again!

MOTHER: Now, don't you carry on. Tell us all about it.

SHEPHERD: You know that cave up there? Well . . . for some time sounds have been coming from that cave. Heavy sighs with grunts mixed up in them. And sometimes snoring, too.

MOTHER: What is it?

SHEPHERD: I'm coming to that. Tonight I crept by the cave and I saw him! As plain as I see you.

MOTHER: Saw whom?

SHEPHERD: Why, *him*, I tell you. He was sitting halfway out of his cave. He was as big as a whale and all covered with scales. He seemed to be daydreaming or something, not raging or snorting.

ROBERT: Scales, did you say?

SHEPHERD: Yes—and claws and a long scaly tail.

ROBERT (*Yawning*): It's all right, Shepherd. Don't worry. It's only a dragon.

MOTHER *and* SHEPHERD (*Shocked*): Only a dragon?

SHEPHERD: How do you know?

MOTHER: Robert knows a great deal about creatures from reading books.

ROBERT: I always said that cave up there was a dragon cave. I would have been surprised if you'd told me it *didn't* have a dragon in it.

SHEPHERD (*Shrieking*): *Do something!*

ROBERT: Tomorrow morning, if I'm free, I'll go up there and have a talk with him. Now, please don't worry. You

don't understand dragons—they're very sensitive, you
know.

MOTHER: Robert's quite right. Now you go home, Shepherd,
and everything will be all right. Won't it, Robert?

ROBERT: Yes, Mother.

SHEPHERD: Oh, me—oh, my. . . . (*He exits. Curtain.*)

* * *

Scene Two

TIME: *The next day.*

SETTING: *Up on the Downs. The opening of the cave is at
right. There is a group of rocks at center, with a book of
poems on it.*

AT RISE: ROBERT *enters and calls.*

ROBERT (*Calling*): Dra-a-a-gon! Oh, Mr. Dragon!

DRAGON (*From offstage; mildly*): Someone come to call?
(DRAGON *enters.*)

ROBERT: I'm only a boy from the nearby town.

DRAGON: Now don't you throw stones or anything. You
must never do that. I'm very sensitive.

ROBERT: I won't. (*He sits down on rock, center stage.*)

DRAGON: Oh—all right.

ROBERT: I've simply come to meet you and ask how you are,
but if I'm bothering you I'll go.

DRAGON: No—no, don't. Really, I'm happy up here, but it is
a bit dull at times.

ROBERT: Going to stay here long?

DRAGON: I just don't know. To tell you the truth, I'm lazy.
Other dragons are so active—always raging and scourging
the countryside, digesting damsels, running after knights

and all—but I like to eat my meals on time, then sleep a bit. I like this country and I'd like to live here.

ROBERT: What do you think about up here by yourself?

DRAGON: Well, I guess it's all right to tell you. (*Shyly*) Did you ever—just for fun—try to write poetry?

ROBERT: Sure I have. Some of it pretty good, too. Only there's no one who'll listen to it.

DRAGON: That's the way it is with me. I'd like to read some of my poems for you and your friends sometime. Listen to this one (*Recites*):

> The pretty clouds go drifting by,
> Up in yonder pale blue sky.
> The warm sun shines on daffodils,
> Giving me such pleasant thrills.

I can dance, too. Watch this. (DRAGON *does a funny dance, finishing with his end in the air.*)

ROBERT: Very interesting—but you don't quite realize your position. (DRAGON *sees his position and straightens up.*)

DRAGON (*Laughing awkwardly*): Qh!

ROBERT: You're an enemy of the people, you see.

DRAGON: Nonsense! Haven't got an enemy in the world.

ROBERT: Oh, dear. I wish you'd try to understand. They'll come after you with sharp sticks and swords. According to them you're a terrible monster.

DRAGON: Not a word of truth to it.

ROBERT: Well, try to be sensible. And do try to act more fearful, the way a dragon should, or you'll find yourself in a terrible situation. (*Standing*) Goodbye for now.

DRAGON: Do come again. I'll miss your company. (ROBERT *exits. Curtain.*)

* * *

Scene Three

SETTING: *The village street.*

AT RISE: MRS. SMYTHE, *the town gossip, is talking to* MOTHER.

MRS. SMYTHE: Oh, it's terrible! The Shepherd told me all about that horrible, dreadful creature up on the Downs. We'll all be eaten alive.

MOTHER: Well, my son went up there this morning, and—

MRS. SMYTHE: You'll never see him again. He's lost forever! Oh, you poor woman. My heart goes out to you . . . but none of us are safe.

ROBERT (*Entering*): Good morning, Mrs. Smythe.

MRS. SMYTHE: Robert! You didn't go up there, did you? Thank heavens.

ROBERT: Up where? Up on the Downs? Sure.

MRS. SMYTHE: And was the monster asleep?

ROBERT: He's no monster. He's a nice fellow, that dragon.

MRS. SMYTHE: A *dragon!* (*She screams and faints on the street.*)

MOTHER: Was he really, Robert? That's nice. Did you have a talk with him?

ROBERT: Yes. He'd like to read us some of his poetry soon.

MRS. SMYTHE (*Sitting up, then standing*): A dragon! I thought it might be. Well, thank heavens I sent the Shepherd to find St. George, the dragon killer, and bring him to this town. We'll be saved.

ROBERT: You don't understand. This dragon likes poetry.

MRS. SMYTHE (*Ignoring him*): He must be exterminated right away.

MOTHER: I had better get dinner started. (*She exits.*)

MRS. SMYTHE: St. George will soon be here to free our suffering village and win fame and renown.

ROBERT: But our village is not suffering! (*Music is heard from offstage*) In fact—

SHEPHERD (*Running in*): Mrs. Smythe! St. George is approaching!

MRS. SMYTHE: Oh, dear. And the streets aren't decorated. Quickly. Let's get the flags and banners out. Robert! Don't just stand there! *Do something!* (MRS. SMYTHE *and* SHEPHERD *exit.*)

ROBERT: Guess I'll go back up on the Downs and warn my friend. (*He exits. Music grows louder. Banners and flags are lowered over stage. One banner reads* WELCOME ST. GEORGE. MRS. SMYTHE, SHEPHERD *and* MOTHER *enter. Cheers and crowd noises are heard from offstage, and* ST. GEORGE *enters on his horse.*)

ST. GEORGE: Friends, Romans, countrymen! No—not that one. (*Pauses, then brightly*) Ah! Four score and twenty years ago . . . No. Er . / . . 'twas the night before Christmas and all through the house. Hm-m-m? (*Looks about*)

MRS. SMYTHE: Welcome to our town, most respected St. George. Save us from a most despicable scourge! There is a terrible dragon up on our Downs.

ST. GEORGE: Have no hear. That's why I'm fear. (*Shakes head*) No, that's not right. A dragon, huh? Just my business. Be glad he's not down on your ups. (*Laughs*) Heh, heh!

SHEPHERD: He's living in a cave. I'll take you to the edge of town and point the way.

ST. GEORGE: Well . . . there's no pime like the tresent. Ah. . . . No time like the present. I'll go up there right away and look into this little matter.

MRS. SMYTHE: Our hero!

MOTHER: While you're up there, please tell my son, Robert, to come home for lunch.

ST. GEORGE: Right-o. Well, off I go.

SHEPHERD: Have faith and courage.

MRS. SMYTHE: Godspeed.

ALL: Goodbye! Goodbye! (ST. GEORGE *exits on his horse. Curtain.*)

*   *   *

Scene Four

SETTING: *The same as Scene 2.*

AT RISE: DRAGON *is onstage.*

DRAGON: I must try this poem before I recite it for the boy and his friends. (*Reads from book*)

Flowers bright, tasteful sight,
Blooming in the sun's strong light.
Red and ocher, blue and white,
They fade away into the night.

That's not bad—although I've written better. (ROBERT *runs in.*)

ROBERT: Dragon! Now you're in for it. He's coming. You'll have to get ready and *do* something.

DRAGON: Don't be so excited, boy. Sit down and get your breath and then perhaps you'll tell me who's coming.

ROBERT: It's *only* St. George, the dragon killer, that's who.

DRAGON: Oh, dear me! This is dreadful. I won't talk to him, and that's that. You must tell him not to come. Say he can send a note, but I won't see him.

ROBERT: Now, Dragon. Don't be stubborn. You've got to

fight him some time or other. Better do it now and then we can get on with our poems.

DRAGON: My dear boy, try to understand. I won't fight. I've never fought and I'm not going to start now.

ROBERT: But if you don't, he'll kill you!

DRAGON: Oh, I don't think so. You'll arrange something, I'm sure. I leave it up to you. (DRAGON *exits into cave*.)

ROBERT (*To himself*): What do I do now? (ST. GEORGE *enters*.)

ST. GEORGE: Hello there, young fellow. Have you seen a dragon about?

ROBERT: He's over in that cave, but he's not about to come out.

ST. GEORGE: Won't come out?

ROBERT: No. You see, St. George, he's a *perfect* dragon.

ST. GEORGE: I quite understand. A villain worthy of my sword.

ROBERT: No! He's not bad. He's a kind, loving sort of dragon. A real gentleman.

ST. GEORGE: Oh? Perhaps I've misjudged him. Just tell him I'd like to talk to him, then. I promise him no harm. Just want to discuss matters.

ROBERT: Well—I'll try. (*Calls into cave*) Dragon! Yoo-hoo!

DRAGON (*From offstage*): I'm busy. Another time.

ROBERT (*To* ST. GEORGE): Perhaps you'd better go away.

ST. GEORGE: Quite impossible! It's against the rules.

ROBERT: Well—let's try to talk to him. (ROBERT *goes to cave again and calls*.) Dragon! Please come out! St. George and I would like to talk to you. (DRAGON *enters from cave*.)

DRAGON (*Speaking quickly*): So glad to meet you, St. George. Perhaps sometime when you can stay longer I can recite for you. Good day. (*He starts to leave*.)

St. George: I think we'd better try to settle this little affair right away and wight it fout—er . . . fight it out.

Robert: Yes—do! It'll save such a lot of bother.

Dragon: My young friend, you stay out of this. The whole thing is nonsense. I'm not going to fight and that's that!

St. George: But this would be a beautiful place to fight. Your beautiful scales rippling and my shining armor glittering in the sun.

Dragon: Now you're trying to get to me through my artistic senses. (*Thoughtfully*) Not that it wouldn't make a pretty picture.

Robert: Good—we seem to be getting down to business.

St. George: The fight can be fixed. I could stab you so that it wouldn't hurt you a bit. How about here? (*He touches* Dragon *on his chest with sword.*)

Dragon (*Laughing*): I'm ticklish. No, not there. I'm bound to laugh.

St. George: How about under the neck—here! (*Touches him under neck.*)

Dragon: That's a good place. Are you sure you can do it right?

St. George: Sure—just leave it to me.

Dragon: All right. Your plan seems like a good one. Let's do it.

Robert: St. George, just what is the Dragon going to get out of this?

St. George: Well—I'm supposed to lead him down the street in triumph.

Robert: And then?

St. George: There'll be shouting and speeches.

Robert: And then what?

Dragon (*Interrupting*): A lovely banquet! Yes, I'll go

through with it. This means I'll be recognized by society at last.

ST. GEORGE: Can you ramp and breathe fire and rage?

DRAGON: I know I can ramp and rage, but I'm a bit out of practice as far as fire-breathing is concerned. I'll do my best.

ST. GEORGE: Good. There has to be a princess—terror-stricken and chained to a rock and all that sort of thing.

ROBERT: Mother will surely help us out. Now I must go home, or Mother will worry. (*To* DRAGON) It's all arranged. First thing in the morning.

DRAGON: Not too early. I'm not my best in the morning. I must get my sleep. Goodbye, Robert. And goodbye, St. George.

ST. GEORGE: 'Bye 'bye. . . . (ROBERT *and* ST. GEORGE *start out.*)

DRAGON (*Calling after them*): And may the best man win! (*Laughs and re-enters cave as curtains close.*)

*   *   *

Scene Five

SETTING: *The same as Scene 2.*

AT RISE: DRAGON *is vocalizing and polishing scales on his chest with his paw.* ROBERT *and his* MOTHER *enter.*

ROBERT: Good morning, Dragon.

DRAGON: Good morning, boy. How do I look? I've been polishing my scales.

ROBERT: Beautiful. Just beautiful. This is my mother.

DRAGON: And a good good morning to you, ma'am.

MOTHER: I hope I can be of service.

DRAGON: Oh, you'll do just fine. Not too dramatic, now. Be realistic—like this (*He overacts*)—HELP! HELP ME! OOOO! SAVE ME FROM THE DRAGON! OOOO!

MOTHER: I get the general idea.

DRAGON: Good. Oh, I hear them coming. I'll go into the cave. (*To himself*) Oh, dear . . . and without a rehearsal! I hope the fight goes well. (*Exits into cave*)

MOTHER (*To* ROBERT): I must say he is a different sort of dragon, dear. I'll stand over here and look distressed. (*She stands near cave. Crowd noises are heard from offstage.* MRS. SMYTHE *and the* SHEPHERD *enter and stand center, behind rocks.*)

MRS. SMYTHE: Oooh! How exciting! We will finally rid ourselves of this terrible monster. Stay near me, Shepherd, and protect me.

SHEPHERD (*Shaking with fright*): Y-y-yes, Mrs. Smythe. I'll pro-pro-protect you. (*He hides behind her.* ST. GEORGE *rides in on his horse. Cheering is heard from offstage.*)

ROBERT (*To himself*): I hope this goes right. Maybe we should have had a run-through. (DRAGON *re-enters, snorting and carrying on furiously. All gasp.*) It looks as if he's as good an actor as he is a poet. (DRAGON *and* ST. GEORGE *begin to fight. There is much shouting and snorting.*)

DRAGON (*Ad lib*): Ramp, ramp! Rage, rage! Snort, snort! Scourge, scourge! (*Etc.*)

ST. GEORGE (*Fiercely*): That'll teach you. Take that! (*Swings at* DRAGON *with sword.* DRAGON *falls to ground in an emotional dying scene. He moans, groans, thrashes about, and at last gives a loud hiss and lies still. All cheer.*)

MRS. SMYTHE *and* SHEPHERD (*Together*): Hooray!

SHEPHERD: Aren't you going to cut his head off?

St. George: I think not. Let's all go down to the town and celebrate instead. I'm sure he'll be a very good dragon from now on. The maiden is saved.

Mother (*Very casually*): I'm saved.

St. George: The town is saved.

Mrs. Smythe: We're all saved. Hail to St. George!

All: Hail to St. George! Hip hip, hoorah! (Mother, Mrs. Smythe *and* Shepherd *exit.*)

Robert: You can get up now, Dragon. (Dragon *gets up.*)

Dragon: I'm a bit dusty and sore.

St. George: That was a fine job of fighting. Some of the most beautiful action I've ever seen out of a dragon.

Dragon: Do you really think so? Perhaps I should go into acting.

Robert: Well, we had better get down to the village.

St. George: Ah, yes. We must hear the speeches!

Dragon: I'll recite a poem I've written for the occasion:

> St. George and the Dragon
> Fought up on the Downs.
> People came to see
> From villages and towns.
>
> The fight was a fair one,
> As all could tell.
> Here's fame to St. George.
> All's well that ends well.

(*They all exit together as curtain closes.*)

THE END

Production Notes

THE RELUCTANT DRAGON

Puppets: 6 hand puppets or marionettes.

Costumes: The Dragon can be a hand puppet with a moving mouth, or a sock puppet. He can have one large hand to help him emote (the puppeteer's other hand in a matching glove), and a long tail to flick about. If he is a marionette, make him big and funny-looking. For a fire-breathing effect, put a rubber tube or straw in his mouth and blow talcum powder through it. St. George should be short and dumpy, with a big walrus moustache and armor. He carries a sword in his hand at all times. His horse can be modeled after a theatrical hobbyhorse and worn over his hips. If it is a marionette show, build a full marionette horse for St. George to ride.

Properties: Book; bowl and spoon for Mother.

Setting: Scene 1, a kitchen interior in an English cottage, is a simple painted backdrop. Scenes 2, 4, and 5: Up on the Downs: backdrop shows rolling hills. There are several rocks, at center, and a cave entrance (a cut-out) at right. Scene 3: The village street. Half-timbered buildings and shops are painted on backdrop. Banners are suspended from above stage, including one reading WELCOME ST. GEORGE.

Lighting: No special effects.

Sound: Crowd noises and cheering, as indicated in text.

JACK AND THE BEANSTALK

Characters

JACK
CHARLOTTE THE COW
BUTTERFLY
MOTHER
HAWKER
MRS. GIANT
MR. GIANT
MAGIC HEN
MAGIC HARP (PRINCESS MELODY)

Scene One

SETTING: *The garden of Jack's house.*
AT RISE: CHARLOTTE THE COW *is posing for* JACK, *who stands at his easel, drawing her.* BUTTERFLY *flies by.*

JACK (*Singing*):
        Old MacDonald had a farm,
        Eee-i, eee-i, oh,
        And on this farm he had a cow,
        Eee-i, eee-i, oh.
        With a—
Cow: Moo! Moo!
JACK (*Continuing song*):
        —here, and a—
Cow: Moo! Moo!
JACK (*Continuing song*):
        —there, here a—

MOTHER (*Calling from offstage*): Jack! What are you doing? Are you at your chores? Charlotte needs milking!

JACK: Charlotte is posing, Mother. (MOTHER *enters from house.*)

MOTHER: Posing? Are you drawing again? Put that silly easel away.

JACK: But, Mother, what makes the sky so blue? And why are butterflies' wings so colorful?

MOTHER: Jack, Jack, why do you always act like such a dumb-dumb when there's so much work to do? The landlord is coming to collect the rent tomorrow and here you are—playing with those useless crayons.

JACK: But, Mama, I like to draw.

MOTHER: Ever since your papa died we have grown poorer and poorer, and now we have no more money left at all. If we don't pay Mr. Bill Overdue, the landlord, we will be sent to the poorhouse! (*Sobs*)

JACK: Don't cry, Mama. Maybe I can sell my drawings.

MOTHER: Those useless things! (*She throws easel offstage.*) No! Take Charlotte to the county fair and sell her.

COW: *Mooooo!*

MOTHER: Yes, you, Charlotte!

JACK: Oh, no. Not Charlotte! Who will pose for me?

MOTHER: Never mind that. The cow must go. But come straight home. It is not safe to be out after dark. Just the other day the Princess was carried off, and goodness knows what has happened to her.

JACK: All right, Mother. Come along, Charlotte. (*He starts off, leading* Cow.)

COW (*Sadly*): Mooooo.

MOTHER: And get a good sum of money for her!

JACK: Goodbye, Mother.

MOTHER: Goodbye, Jack.

Cow (*Saying goodbye*): Moo-ooo! (*Jack leads* Cow *off and* Mother *exits. Curtain.*)

* * *

Scene Two

Setting: *At the fair. This scene is played before the curtain. Hawker's table is at center. There are three shells on it. There is a bag of beans on ground.*
At Rise: Hawker *stands behind table, calling.*

Hawker: Hurry! Hurry! See the shell game! (Jack *enters with* Cow *and they stand close to* Hawker.) Step aside, little man. (*Calling*) Try to guess which shell holds the magic beans. (*To* Jack) Go away, little boy. You bother me. (*Calls*) Hurry! Hurry! (Cow *eats bag of beans, making munching sounds. To* Jack) Your cow just ate my magic beans! She ate the whole bagful.
Jack: I'm sorry. But she was hungry!
Cow: Mooooo!
Hawker: Hungry, smungry. That's no excuse. I have only three magic beans left. You'll have to pay for the ones your cow ate.
Jack: But I have no money. All I have is this cow.
Hawker: Well, I'll tell you what I'm goin' to do. To show you my heart is in the right purse—er—place, I'm going to *give* you the last three magic beans, in exchange for your cow. (*Gives beans to* Jack)
Jack: Well—that seems fair. Mother will be pleased with these magic beans. They *are* magic, aren't they?
Hawker: Why, certainly. You don't think I'd cheat you, do you?

JACK: Oh, no. Well, I must go home now. Thank you, and goodbye. (HAWKER *begins to lead* Cow *off.*)
Cow: Mooooo. . . .
JACK: Goodbye, Charlotte. (JACK *exits. Curtain.*)

* * *

Scene Three

SETTING: *The same as Scene 1.*
AT RISE: JACK *enters, carrying beans.*

JACK: Mother! I'm home.
MOTHER (*Entering*): Oh, there you are, Jack. Did you get a good price for the cow?
JACK: Yes. I met the strangest man at the fair. And in exchange for Charlotte he gave me these three magic beans. (*Gives her beans*) Aren't you proud of me?
MOTHER: Oh, Jack! How could you? What a dumb-dumb you are!
JACK: But these are magic beans.
MOTHER: Ridiculous! How can you be so gullible? (*Throws beans down*) *That* for your beans! Now go right to bed. There's nothing to eat for supper, anyway. (*Moans*) What shall we do? What shall we do? (MOTHER *and* JACK *exit. At rear, a huge beanstalk begins to grow up from below stage, slowly growing up past top of stage, out of sight. Lights dim to indicate passage of time. Sound of rooster crowing is heard from offstage.* JACK *enters, stretching.*)
JACK: Oh, what a good sleep I had. It's such a beautiful morning. Now I must find a way to earn some money. (*He sees beanstalk.*) What's this? I can't believe my eyes. The magic

beans have grown up to the sky. They were magic beans, after all. (*He starts to climb beanstalk.* MOTHER *enters.*)

MOTHER: Jack! What are you doing up there? Where did that beanstalk come from? Come back!

JACK (*Still climbing*): I'll be back soon, Mother. Don't worry about me. The beans were magic, after all. (*Curtain.*)

*   *   *

Scene Four

SETTING: *At the door of the Giant's castle. Door is at center, before curtain. This scene is played in front of curtain.*

AT RISE: JACK *enters.*

JACK: I've been climbing for the longest time—right up into the clouds. And now I've come to a giant-sized castle. I'll just knock on the door and see who lives here. (*He knocks, waits.*) I'll knock harder. (*Knocks harder.*)

MRS. GIANT (*Opening door and looking out*): Mercy me! I thought I heard someone knocking but I don't see anyone here!

JACK (*Calling*): Here I am. Down here!

MRS. GIANT (*Not hearing him*): I guess I was imagining things. (*Slams door*)

JACK (*Knocking again*): Let me in!

MRS. GIANT (*Opening door*): I *did* hear a knocking. I'll bet it's that pesky raven knocking at my door.

JACK (*Shouting*): NO! IT'S ME! LOOK DOWN HERE!

MRS. GIANT: I don't—(*Sees him*) Oh! There is a little man on the doorstep. (*To* JACK) My, my. You are a little one.

You had better leave quickly or my husband, the Giant, will eat you for dinner.

JACK: Please let me in. I'm so hungry and tired from that long climb.

MRS. GIANT: Well! You do look undernourished. Come in and I'll give you some crumbs from the table.

JACK: Oh, thank you.

MRS. GIANT: But don't make any noise, for if the Giant finds you here it will be certain doom. You will be food for him. (JACK *enters, closing door behind him, and follows* MRS. GIANT *offstage, or through split in curtain.*)

*　　*　　*

Scene Five

SETTING: *The Giant's kitchen. An oversized table stands at center. Giant-sized stove is at rear, with dishes of food on it.*

AT RISE: MRS. GIANT *puts* JACK *on table.*

MRS. GIANT: Just sit here on the table. (*Pointing to tabletop*) Here are some crumbs.

JACK: Oh, thank you. You are so kind. (*Loud stamping noises are heard from offstage.*)

MRS. GIANT: I hear my husband, Mr. Giant, coming. Quickly! Hide! (JACK *hides under table.*)

MR. GIANT (*From offstage*): Fee, fi, fo, fum. I smell the blood of a little dumb-dumb. (GIANT *enters.*) I smell the presence of a stranger. Has anyone been here today?

MRS. GIANT: Don't be silly. You only smell the mutton stew in the oven.

GIANT: Well, it sure smells like a dumb-dumb to me. Give me my dinner, woman.

MRS. GIANT (*Going to stove for food*): Here you are—mutton (*Slams dish on table*), bread (*Places bread on table*), and cheese. (*Puts cheese on table.*)

GIANT: I sure am hungry. Now for the mutton. (*Eats*) Yum, yum! (JACK *stands, quickly takes bread, and hides under table again, unseen by* GIANT) That sure is good mutton! (*Looks for bread*) Where's that loaf of bread?

MRS. GIANT: Er . . . you ate it.

GIANT: I did? I don't remember. Hm-m-m. Guess I did. (*Eats more mutton*) Yum, yum! (JACK *takes cheese.*) Now for the cheese. (*Looks for cheese*) Why, it's gone! The cheese is gone!

MRS. GIANT: A mouse ate it!

GIANT: He did? Hm-m-m. Well, back to the mutton. Where's the pepper?

MRS. GIANT: Here! (*Hands him pepper shaker from stove.*)

GIANT: I like lots of pepper on my mutton. (*Shakes pepper generously.* JACK *sneezes.*) What was that?

MRS. GIANT: Just the cat sneezing. She has a cold.

GIANT: Oh. Now bring me my money. (MRS. GIANT *exits and re-enters with bag of gold coins.*)

MRS. GIANT: Here it is. (*She hands him bag and exits.*)

GIANT: Now to count my gold. (*Spills few coins out of bag onto table and starts to count them*) One, two, three, five—er—one, two, three—uh—six? That's not right. This is so hard! It makes me sleepy. I'll just take a little snooze. (GIANT *falls asleep and snores.*) Zzz-z-z-z-z-z.

JACK (*Coming out from under table*): Oh, look at all that money! (MRS. GIANT *enters.*) How pleased my mother would be if we had but a few gold coins to keep us from starving.

MRS. GIANT: Oh, you poor people! (*Hands bag of coins to* JACK) Here! Take the whole bag. My husband will never miss it. He has eleventy-seven more bags under his mattress.

JACK: Why, thank you! I'll never forget—

GIANT (*Waking up*): Ho-hum. (*Yawns*)

MRS. GIANT: Quick! Hide again! (JACK *hides under table.*)

GIANT: Wife, there's a thief in the house! My gold is missing.

MRS. GIANT: Don't be silly. I just put it back under your mattress so it would be safe.

GIANT: Well, I need more gold to fill that last bag, so bring me my Magic Hen that lays the golden eggs.

MRS. GIANT: Yes, dear. (*She exits and re-enters with* MAGIC HEN, *puts* HEN *on table and exits.*)

HEN: Cluck, cluck, cluck—

GIANT: Magic Hen, lay more golden eggs or I shall wring your neck.

HEN (*Loudly*): Cluck! Cluck! (*She lays golden egg.*)

GIANT: More! More golden eggs!

HEN: Cluck! Cluck! Cluck! (*Lays more eggs*)

GIANT: Good. That should be enough. I'm sleepy from all that hard work. (*He falls asleep again.*) Zzz-z-z-z. (JACK *comes out from under table again.*)

HEN: Cluck! Cluck! Jack! Please take me away with you. The Giant is so cruel to me. Cluck! Cluck! I'm sure he will kill me when I cannot lay enough eggs to satisfy his greed for gold. He grows more greedy every day. Oh, dear! Cluck-cluck-cluck!

JACK: I'll take you with me, Hen.

HEN: Oh, thank you, dear boy! Cluck! Cluck!

GIANT (*Waking up*): Ho-hum!

HEN: Let's hide. He's waking up. (*They hide under table.* MRS. GIANT *enters.*)

GIANT: What was that noise? I heard someone in here.

MRS. GIANT: Nonsense, dear. You were only having a bad dream.

GIANT: Well, I can't get back to sleep in this noisy castle. Bring me my Magic Harp. Maybe her soothing voice will make me sleep again.

MRS. GIANT: Yes, dear. (*Exits and re-enters at once with* MAGIC HARP, *which she puts down beside table.*) Here's your Magic Harp. Now, sleep tight.

GIANT: Play, Harp! Play! I command you! (*Harp music is heard from offstage.*)

HARP (*Chanting*):

　　　Although you have me in your spell,
　　　There must be someone I can tell.
　　　I'm really not a harp, you see,
　　　For I am Princess Melody.

GIANT (*Falling asleep*): Zzz-z-z-z-z-z-z.

JACK (*Coming out again*): Could it be true? Can this Harp really be the Princess Melody under an evil spell? (*To* HARP) How can I save you?

HARP (*Chanting*):

　　　You must escape the Giant's house,
　　　And be as quiet as a mouse.
　　　Take me with you when you flee,
　　　Or else there'll be no hope for me.

JACK: Of course, I'll take you with me. We'll go right away, before the Giant wakes. I'll just pick up the Hen (*Takes* HEN *from table*), and now you, Harp (*Takes* HARP), and now the bag of gold. . . . (*Drops bag. Coins spill with a clatter.* JACK *starts to exit, with* HEN *and* HARP, *abandoning gold coins.*)

GIANT (*Waking up*): What was that? (*Looks around*)

Someone has stolen my Magic Hen! (*Sees* JACK) There he goes with my Magic Hen and my Magic Harp! (*Chases* JACK *around and around stage*)

HEN (*Ad lib*): Hurry, Jack! Cluck, cluck! Hurry! Squawk! (*Etc.*)

HARP (*Chanting*):

>Now just see what you have done!
>You've spilled the gold coins, one by one.
>He's now awake and chasing us.
>I never have heard such a fuss.

MRS. GIANT: No, husband! Don't hurt him! He's so small. He will only give you indigestion! (JACK *exits with* HEN *and* HARP, *followed by* GIANT. *Curtain*)

*   *   *

Scene Six

SETTING: *Jack's garden, the same as Scene 1.*

AT RISE: JACK *is coming down the beanstalk with* HARP *and* HEN.

JACK (*Calling*): Mother!

MOTHER (*Entering*): What are you doing up there? Come down, Jack! You'll hurt yourself.

JACK: Quickly! Get an ax! (*Jumps off beanstalk, puts down* HEN *and* HARP)

MOTHER: This is no time to chop wood. Where have you been?

JACK: Mother, the Giant is coming!

MOTHER (*Terrified*): I'll do it! I'll get the ax! (*Exits and re-enters at once with ax*) I'll do it!

JACK: Please, Mother! I'd rather do it myself. (*He takes ax and chops at beanstalk.*)

GIANT (*From offstage*): Fee, fi, fo, fum! Wait till I catch that little dumb-dumb!

MOTHER: Hurry, Jack! Hurry! I can see his boots already!

JACK (*Still chopping*): I'm chopping as fast as I can. (*Chops again. Beanstalk falls to ground. GIANT shouts offstage, as if falling. There is a loud thud from offstage. MOTHER screams and hides her eyes.*) Mother, you can look now. It's all right—the Giant has fallen through the ground.

MOTHER: Oh, dear! He fell right through my cabbage patch. (*Sound of chord played on harp is heard from offstage. HARP is quickly removed and PRINCESS MELODY appears in its place.*)

JACK: Look what I've brought back, Mother. A Magic Hen, a Magic Harp (*Sees PRINCESS*)—er . . .

MOTHER: It's the Princess Melody!

JACK: Why, Princess. The spell is broken! You are no longer a harp.

PRINCESS: Thank you for rescuing me, Jack.

JACK (*Shyly*): It was nothing. Mother, I'm afraid I dropped the gold I was bringing back to you.

HEN: Never fear! Cluck, cluck. For if you will let me live here with you and your mother, I will gladly lay enough golden eggs to take care of all your needs.

MOTHER: You can move in right away.

PRINCESS: Now I must go home to my father, the King.

JACK: I will take you to your castle. Before we leave, I would like you to have this picture I drew of Charlotte. She was my friend. (*Hands her picture of Cow from easel*)

PRINCESS (*Looking at picture*): Why, Jack. You are a fine artist. You must continue painting. I didn't know you loved horses.

MOTHER: But, Charlotte's not—

JACK (*Quickly*): We'd better leave before it gets dark.

MOTHER: Come right home, Jack. We're having beans for supper.

JACK: Magic beans? (*All laugh.*)

MOTHER: Goodbye, Princess Melody.

PRINCESS: Goodbye. (PRINCESS *and* JACK *exit.*)

MOTHER: Well—maybe my boy, Jack, isn't such a dumb-dumb after all! (*Curtain.*)

THE END

Production Notes

JACK AND THE BEANSTALK

Number of Puppets: 10 hand puppets, rod puppets, or marionettes, or a combination. If desired, the Giants can be played by a boy and girl, instead of puppets. The actors stand in front of the puppet stage and use the stage apron for the kitchen table in Scene 5.

Playing Time: 15 minutes.

Description of Puppets: Jack and his mother wear shabby clothes with patches. Hawker is a sort of W. C. Fields character, with a top hat and tie. Mr. and Mrs. Giant are larger than other puppets or marionettes. Princess has a little crown, and flowing gown and robe. Harp is painted gold.

Properties: Beans, dish of mutton, cheese, bag containing gold coins, golden eggs, pepper shaker, harp, ax, and drawing of Cow.

Setting: Scenes 1, 3, and 6: The garden of Jack's house. There are flowers and one or two trees placed around stage. Jack's easel is downstage, with drawing on it. Jack's house is shown at rear, to one side. NOTE: Beanstalk can be made of paper or stiff cloth leaves sewn to a rope, which is pulled up on a heavy thread, through a screw eye or other holder above the stage. In Scene 6, release the thread quickly when Jack chops down the beanstalk. Scene 2: A fair. This scene is played before curtain. Hawker's table is center. Scene 4: At the door of Giant's castle. Door frame with working door is at center. Frame is made without a top, so that marionettes can walk through the frame when door is opened. The door can also be omitted, if necessary, and assumed to be offstage. Scene 5: Giant's kitchen, in the castle. An oversized table stands at center. Stove, also giant-sized, stands at rear. It holds dish of mutton, loaf of bread, cheese, and pepper shaker. Cloth covers table so Jack can hide beneath it. NOTE: If actors take parts of Giants, they stand in front of puppet stage and use the stage apron for the kitchen table. Food properties and bag of gold coins can then be easily handled by actors. If marionettes are used, put the hand properties on rods made of straightened coat hangers so that they can be manipulated from above.

Lighting: No special effects.

Sound: Harp music, as indicated in text. Music may also be played between scenes.

THE TINDERBOX

Adapted from a story by Hans Christian Andersen

Characters

SOLDIER
WITCH
INNKEEPER
DOG WITH EYES AS BIG AS SAUCERS
DOG WITH EYES AS BIG AS MILLSTONES
DOG WITH EYES AS BIG AS THE ROUND TOWER
PRINCESS PATRICIA
KING
EXECUTIONER
BOY
NARRATOR

Scene One

SETTING: *A dusty road near an inn. There is a large gnarled tree center stage.*

AT RISE: SOLDIER *enters, walking along road.*

NARRATOR: Once upon a time there was a soldier who was marching along the highroad. He had a knapsack on his back and his sword at his side, for he had been to the wars and now was on his way home, although, alas, he really had no home to return to. . . .

SOLDIER: Hup, two! One, two! (WITCH *jumps out from behind tree.*)

WITCH: Ho there, Soldier! Are you returning from the wars?

SOLDIER: Why, yes, old woman.

WITCH: My—you are a *real* soldier—with your big knapsack and such a nice sword! I foresee that you will have as much money as ever you like!

SOLDIER: Thank you kindly, old woman. Are you a fortune teller?

WITCH: Yes, you might say that. Do you see that tree yonder?

SOLDIER: You mean this big one here? (*He crosses to tree.*)

WITCH: Yes. It is hollow inside. Come, I will show you. (*She shows him back of tree.*) See this hole in the back? If you will crawl in and let yourself down into the cave under the tree, I will tie a rope around your waist so that I can pull you up again when you call.

SOLDIER: Why? What am I to do down there under the tree, old woman?

WITCH: Fetch money—that's what! When you get to the bottom you will find yourself in a wide passage with three boxes in the middle of the floor.

SOLDIER: How will I see them?

WITCH: The passage is quite light—have no fear. On top of each box is a dog—the first dog with eyes as big as saucers; the second with eyes as big as millstones; and the third with eyes as big as the Round Tower. The first box contains copper; the second, silver; and the third, gold. Take as much money as you like.

SOLDIER: But what about the dogs?

WITCH: Oh, never fear them. Just take this magic apron (*She gives her apron to him.*), place it over each dog, and he will fall asleep immediately. Then you can take as much money from the boxes as you like.

SOLDIER: That doesn't sound so hard. But what am I to bring you? Surely, you'll want something!

WITCH: No, not a single penny do I want, for money has brought me naught but grief. But, if you wish, you can bring me an old tinderbox that my grandmother forgot the last time she was down there.

SOLDIER: Hm-m-m-m. Well, tie the rope around me, and in I go.

WITCH: Come in back of the tree. (*They go behind the tree, out of view of the audience.*) There! And here is the apron. (WITCH *appears.*) Are you ready?

SOLDIER (*From behind tree*): Here I go! (WITCH *peers behind tree.*)

WITCH: Are you down yet?

SOLDIER (*In cave; muffled voice*): Yes. And I see the three dogs.

WITCH: Well, get on with it.

SOLDIER (*From cave*): I've put your apron over the fierce dogs, and they are asleep.

WITCH: The tinderbox—do you see the tinderbox?

SOLDIER (*From cave*): Now I've opened the boxes and (*Whistles in admiration*)—there sure is a lot of money here!

WITCH: Hurry, before someone comes by. (*To herself*) Oh, what's taking him so long? When I have the tinderbox, I shall turn him into a dog! Heh, heh!

SOLDIER (*From cave*): O.K. You can haul me up now.

WITCH: Have you the tinderbox?

SOLDIER (*From cave*): Oh, to be sure! I haven't forgotten. Pull me up! (WITCH *goes behind tree.*)

WITCH (*Grunting and groaning as if pulling rope up*): Help a little. You are heavy! (SOLDIER *comes out from behind tree, followed by* Witch. Soldier *carries three bags of money, and tinderbox.*)

Soldier: My, that was quite a place. And those dogs! I've never seen their like before!

Witch: Yes, yes—now give me my tinderbox!

Soldier: What do you want with that old box?

Witch: That's no business of yours—you've got your money. Now give me what's mine!

Soldier: Rubbish. You are up to no good, you old witch. Tell me what you want with it or I shall thrash you.

Witch (*Attacking him*): Give it to me!

Soldier: All right, I will! (*He beats* Witch) Take that! And that!

Witch: No! No! (*Shrieking*) Ah-h-h-h-h. . . . (*She runs off.*)

Soldier: I have all this money and an old tinderbox to boot. I think I'll just go to that old inn and order the grandest room and all the fine food that I like! No witch will get the best of me. (*He marches toward inn, counting.*) One, two! One, two! (*He exits. Curtain.*)

*   *   *

Scene Two

Time: *That evening.*

Setting: *Inside a room in the inn.*

At Rise: Innkeeper *is talking to the* Soldier, *now dressed in clean uniform.*

Innkeeper: Will that be all, sir?

Soldier: Yes, thank you, Innkeeper. Your meals here are delicious!

INNKEEPER: Nothing is too good for a gentleman of your standing.

SOLDIER: I like to be comfortable. But I do get rather lonesome.

INNKEEPER: A fine-looking gentleman like yourself should be marrying the King's daughter, Princess Patricia. Now there's a lovely thing.

SOLDIER: Where can I see her?

INNKEEPER: Ah, there's the rub. You can't see her at all. She lives in a great copper castle surrounded by walls and towers. Nobody but the King may go in and out, for it has been prophesied that she will marry a common soldier, and the King doesn't like that!

SOLDIER: I should like to see her, all the same. Is there no way to get into the castle?

INNKEEPER: No, none! Many soldiers have tried, and lost their lives in the attempt. So think no more about it, and you'll be better off. Now I must be going. If you need anything, just ring the bell for service. Good night! (INNKEEPER *leaves*.)

SOLDIER: Now my interest has been aroused! I must meet this Princess—but how? My, it's getting dark in here. I must light the candles! (*Patting his pockets*) Drat—no matches. (*Sees tinderbox on table*) Ah—the old tinderbox. I wonder if it works. We'll see. (*He strikes tinderbox and the* DOG WITH SAUCER EYES *appears at rear*.)

DOG WITH SAUCER EYES: What does my master command?

SOLDIER: By heaven! This is a nice kind of tinderbox, if I can get whatever I want like this. No wonder that old witch wanted it! (*To the* DOG) Bring the Princess Patricia here to my room, so that I may see if she really is as beautiful as they say. (DOG *leaves and returns at once carrying sleeping* PRINCESS.) Such fast service! Ah, she still sleeps.

And such a beauty! I cannot resist—just one small kiss!
(*He kisses her and she stirs.*)

PRINCESS: Ah!

DOG WITH SAUCER EYES: Master, she awakens!

SOLDIER: Quickly—return her to the castle!

DOG WITH SAUCER EYES: No sooner said than done. (*Exits carrying* PRINCESS)

SOLDIER: Oh, such a beauty! I must have her for my wife. Tomorrow, after I have had a good night's sleep, I will have her brought here again, and ask her to marry me. Until then, goodnight, my sweet Princess, wherever you are! (*Curtain*)

*   *   *

Scene Three

SETTING: *It is morning in the same room in the Inn.*

AT RISE: SOLDIER *stands in room. There is a knock at the door.* INNKEEPER *enters.*

INNKEEPER: Good morning! I trust you slept well? It's almost noon, and the entire town is talking about the mysterious goings-on at the castle! It seems Princess Patricia had a dream last night that she was carried off to a strange land where a handsome soldier gave her her first kiss. And now she is madly in love. The King is upset. He plans to double the guard tonight, hoping to catch the trespasser.

SOLDIER: You don't say? Hm-m-m. Very interesting. But leave now. I have work to do.

INNKEEPER: Yes, my lord. Good day. (INNKEEPER *leaves*)

SOLDIER: Now, where did I put that tinderbox? (*Sees it on table*) Oh, yes. Here it is. (*He strikes it twice and the* DOG WITH EYES AS BIG AS MILLSTONES *appears at rear.*)

DOG WITH MILLSTONE EYES: What does my master command?

SOLDIER: Well, if it isn't the second dog, with eyes as big as millstones! Bring the Princess to me.

DOG WITH MILLSTONE EYES: So be it! (*He exits and returns at once with* PRINCESS.)

PRINCESS: Where am I? And who are you? (DOG *exits.*)

SOLDIER: I am just a humble soldier, seeking your hand in marriage.

PRINCESS: Oh! My dream! Then it did happen! Oh, I am so happy.

SOLDIER: You are? Then, will you be my wife?

PRINCESS: I—(*Door opens and the* KING *and* EXECUTIONER *rush in.*)

KING: Seize him! Seize him! And throw him into the dungeons.

SOLDIER (*As* EXECUTIONER *drags him off*): Let me go! Let me go! (*They exit.*)

PRINCESS: Oh, Father! How cruel you are. How did you find me?

KING: Simple. I had a small bag filled with fine grains of buckwheat sewed to the hem of your gown. Then I cut a small hole in the bag and followed the trail of grains to this inn. (*Gives a nasty laugh.*)

PRINCESS (*Weeping*): Boo-hoo! Don't you ever want me to marry?

KING: Certainly not a common soldier. Now, come along. We must get back to the castle so I can watch them build the gallows! For tomorrow your clever soldier will be hanged. (KING *laughs and* PRINCESS *cries as they exit. Curtain.*)

*   *   *

Scene Four

SETTING: *A dungeon cell.*
AT RISE: SOLDIER *paces floor.*

SOLDIER: I'm in a pretty mess! Today I am to be hanged and the only thing that can help me is lying on the table next to my bed at the inn. (*There is a knock on the door.* BOY *enters, carrying a tray.*)

BOY: Here's your breakfast, sir. (*Puts tray down.*)

SOLDIER: Thank you, boy. Now wait! Don't be in such a hurry. How would you like to earn yourself a whole gold piece?

BOY: A *whole* gold piece? How?

SOLDIER: Just run to the Inn and fetch me my tinderbox. The Innkeeper will show you my room. Quickly!

BOY: Yes, sir! Right away! (*He dashes out.*)

SOLDIER: I hope he does not stop along the wayside, or it may be too late for me! (KING *and* EXECUTIONER *enter.*) Good day, Your Majesty. Surely you are going to allow a condemned man a last wish.

KING: Very well. But be quick about it. What is your wish?

SOLDIER: I wish very much to smoke a pipe, as it will be my last.

KING: Executioner! Fetch this soldier a pipe. (EXECUTIONER *exits.*) Ah—this is going to be a beautiful execution. It's dark and gloomy outside. Just right for a hanging. (*He sings.*) Dum de dum dum. . . .

SOLDIER: I wish I could be so happy. (EXECUTIONER *returns with pipe.*)

KING: Here is a pipe for you.

SOLDIER: Alas, I have no matches.

KING: Hm-m-m. Executioner, go get some matches. (EXE-

CUTIONER *leaves again.*) Oh! This is so exciting. We haven't hanged anyone in months! (EXECUTIONER *returns with matches.*) Ah—and here are your matches.

SOLDIER: Well—er—I. . . .

KING: Go on—take them.

SOLDIER: I—I . . . (BOY *enters with the tinderbox.*)

BOY: Here is your tinderbox, sir!

SOLDIER: Aye, and just in time, too. Thank you, boy. (BOY *exits.* SOLDIER *strikes the tinderbox three times and* THREE DOGS *appear.*)

THREE DOGS (*Together*): What is your wish, my lord?

SOLDIER: Save me! Save me from being hanged! (DOG WITH SAUCER EYES *and* DOG WITH MILLSTONE EYES *rush at* KING *and* EXECUTIONER *and drive them away.*)

KING: Ow! Ow! Go away! Help! (*He exits, with* EXECUTIONER. DOGS *run after them.*)

SOLDIER (*To* DOG WITH EYES AS BIG AS THE ROUND TOWER): And you—rush to the tower and bring the Princess Patricia to me!

DOG WITH ROUND TOWER EYES: Yes, my master. (*He leaves and returns at once with* PRINCESS. DOG *exits.*)

PRINCESS: How did I get here? (*To* SOLDIER, *happily*) It's you!

SOLDIER: Yes. I had you brought here so I might ask you once more to. . . .

BOY (*Entering*): Sir! Sir, the King and his guards and the executioner have fled the country. You are free again! Please say you will be our King and marry our beautiful Princess.

SOLDIER: Why, that sounds like a fine idea! (*He laughs.*) Now, why didn't I think of it? (*To* PRINCESS) How does that sound to you? Will you marry me and help me rule the kingdom? And love me forever?

PRINCESS: Oh, yes. With all my heart!

SOLDIER: And you, boy, shall become official tinderbox car-
rier to the King—for I wish always to have this wonderful
tinderbox by my side. (PRINCESS *and* SOLDIER *exit, followed by* BOY, *as* NARRATOR *speaks.*)

NARRATOR: And so, the Soldier and the Princess were married, and the wedding feast lasted eight days. And the Dogs
sat at the table and made eyes at everybody. (*Curtain*)

THE END

Production Notes

THE TINDERBOX

Number of Puppets: 11 hand puppets or marionettes (including two versions of Soldier).

Playing Time: 10 minutes.

Description of Puppets: Make two similar puppets for the Soldier. The first should be in a dusty, shabby uniform, with a knapsack on his back, and a sword by his side. The second puppet looks just like the first, except that he has a fresh, clean uniform, and no knapsack. The Witch has an ugly face, and wears a tattered old dress, like a beggar woman, with an apron over it. The Innkeeper is a rolypoly man with a fat stomach. He wears a white apron. The Princess is very beautiful. She wears a filmy gown, and a small crown. King is elegant but evil. He wears a cape and regal clothes. The Executioner wears an eye mask, and black clothes. Boy wears a shabby jacket and trousers. Three Dogs look alike except for their different sizes—big, huge, and tremendous. They have sparkling round eyes.

Properties: Three bags of money, tinderbox (a metal box with a rough side to strike a piece of flint that is stored inside), tray with a dish on it, pipe, box of matches.

Setting: Scene 1: A dusty country road near the Inn. There is a large, gnarled tree at center, with a rope behind it. Scene 2: Inside the Soldier's room at the Inn. There are a bed and table with a candlestick on one side of room, and a door at other side. Scene 3: The same as Scene 2. Scene 4:

133

A dungeon cell. Bed with rough blanket is at one side. Barred window is at rear, and barred door at front.

Lighting: Dim evening lighting in Scene 2, as indicated.

Sound: Dogs enter and exit with a "zoom" sound effect.

ALICE'S ADVENTURES IN WONDERLAND

Adapted from the book by Lewis Carroll

Characters

NARRATOR
ALICE
ALICE'S SISTER
WHITE RABBIT
FISH FOOTMAN
FROG FOOTMAN
DUCHESS
COOK
BABY
CHESHIRE CAT
MARCH HARE
MAD HATTER
DORMOUSE
QUEEN OF HEARTS
KING OF HEARTS
CARDS

Scene One

SETTING: *A riverbank.*
AT RISE: ALICE'S SISTER *is sitting down, reading from a book to* ALICE, *who sits nearby.*

ALICE'S SISTER:
        A boat, beneath a sunny sky,
        Lingering onward dreamily,

> In an evening of July—
> Children three that nestle near,
> Eager eye and willing ear,
> Pleased a simple tale to hear—

ALICE: Dear sister, I don't really know why you read that book. What use is a book without pictures or conversation? (*To herself*) Oh, dear. This hot day is making me very sleepy. (*She lies down. ALICE'S SISTER exits. WHITE RABBIT runs in, looking at his watch.*)

WHITE RABBIT: Oh, dear! Oh, dear! I shall be late! (*He exits.*)

ALICE: Late? I wonder what for? A rabbit with a waistcoat and watch! Most peculiar. (*She gets up and peers offstage after WHITE RABBIT.*) He's gone down that rabbit hole. I'll just see where he goes. (*She exits. From offstage*) Oh-h-h! I'm falling! (*Curtain*)

*   *   *

Scene Two

SETTING: *In the rabbit hole.*

AT RISE: ALICE *is floating in mid-air. Bookcases and shelves pass by her as she falls.*

ALICE: I seem to be falling down a very deep well. Or else I'm falling very slowly. It's too dark to see where I'm going. All the cupboards and bookshelves are filled. (*Turns*) Let's see—here is some orange marmalade. After such a fall as this I shall think nothing of tumbling down stairs! I wonder how many miles I've fallen by this time? I must be getting somewhere near the center of the earth. I hope they remember to feed Dinah her saucer of milk at tea time. There are no mice in the air, I'm afraid, but you might catch a bat, Dinah. And that's very like a mouse, you know. But do cats eat bats, I wonder? (*She yawns.*) Do cats eat bats? Do cats eat bats? Do bats eat cats? (ALICE *lands on the ground.*) Oh! (*She gets up.*) I don't seem to be a bit hurt from that fall. (*Looks offstage*) Why, there goes the White Rabbit! I'll follow him. (*She runs off, as curtains close.*)

*   *   *

Scene Three

SETTING: *In front of the Duchess's house. There is a doorway, with a sign over it reading,* THE DUCHESS. *This scene may be played before the curtain.*
AT RISE: WHITE RABBIT *runs in.*

RABBIT: Oh, my ears and whiskers, how late it's getting! I'll be late for the Queen's game. She will be furious. (*He exits.* ALICE *runs in.*)
ALICE (*Calling to* RABBIT): Wait! Wait for me! Oh, dear. He's gone again. (*Looks around*) Here's a little house. Perhaps they can help me. (*She watches as* FISH FOOTMAN *enters, carrying large envelope, crosses to door, and knocks.* FROG FOOTMAN *enters, goes to door and opens it.*)
FISH FOOTMAN (*Presenting envelope to* FROG FOOTMAN): For the Duchess. An invitation from the Queen to play croquet. (*They bow and knock heads together. Both fall over backward, then get up.*)
FROG FOOTMAN: For the Duchess. An invitation from the Queen to play croquet. (*They bow again, knock heads, fall over, then get up.* FISH FOOTMAN *exits, as* ALICE

laughs. *She crosses to door. From offstage, sounds of howl-ing, sneezing and crashing are heard.* ALICE *knocks on door.*) There's no sort of use in knocking. And that for two reasons. First, because I'm on the same side of the door as you are. Secondly, because they're making such a noise inside, no one could possibly hear you. (*Offstage noises grow louder.*)

ALICE: Please, then. How am I to get in?

FROG FOOTMAN: There might be some sense in your knock-ing if we had the door between us. For instance, if you were inside, you might knock and I could let you out, you know. (FROG FOOTMAN *sits on stoop of door.*)

ALICE (*More firmly*): How am I to get in?

FROG FOOTMAN: I shall sit here till tomorrow. . . .

ALICE: It's really dreadful the way all the creatures here ar-gue. It's enough to drive one crazy. Oh, there's no use talking to him. (ALICE *enters the door. Curtain.*)

*   *   *

Scene Four

SETTING: *The Duchess's kitchen.*

AT RISE: COOK *is stirring a pot on the stove and sprinkling pepper in it with her other hand.* DUCHESS *is sitting on a stool holding* BABY, *who howls.* CHESHIRE CAT *is sitting on stove.* ALICE *enters and looks around.*

ALICE (*Sneezing*): There's certainly too much pepper in that soup! (*Sneezes again. To* DUCHESS) Please, would you tell me why your cat grins like that?

DUCHESS (*Bouncing* BABY): It's a Cheshire Cat. That's why. (*To* BABY) Pig! (BABY *continues to howl.*)

ALICE: I didn't know that Cheshire Cats always grinned. In fact, I didn't know that cats could grin.

DUCHESS: They all can and most of 'em do.

ALICE: I don't know of any that do.

DUCHESS: You don't know much, and that's a fact. (COOK *suddenly begins to throw pots and pans at* DUCHESS *and* BABY. DUCHESS *ignores them.* BABY *continues to howl.*)

ALICE: Oh, Cook! Please mind what you're doing. There goes the baby's precious nose.

DUCHESS: If everybody minded their own business the world would go 'round a great deal faster than it does.

ALICE (*Brightly*): Which would not be an advantage. Just think what work it would make with the day and night. You see, the Earth takes twenty-four hours to turn round on its axis—

DUCHESS: Talking of axes—chop off her head!

ALICE: Twenty-four hours, I think; or is it twelve?

DUCHESS: Oh, don't bother me. I never could abide figures. (*She sings to the tune of "Pop Goes the Weasel."*)

> Speak roughly to your little boy,
> And beat him when he sneezes.
> He only does it to annoy
> Because he knows it teases.

(*Speaks*) Chorus.

DUCHESS *and* COOK: Wow! Wow! Wow! (DUCHESS *tosses* BABY *in the air.*)

DUCHESS (*Singing again*):

> I speak severely to my boy,
> I beat him when he sneezes,
> For he can thoroughly enjoy
> The pepper when he pleases.

(*Speaks*) Chorus.

DUCHESS *and* COOK: Wow! Wow! Wow!

DUCHESS: Here! (*She hands* BABY *to* ALICE.) You may hold it a bit, if you like! I must go get ready to play croquet with the Queen. (ALICE *takes* BABY *and exits.* DUCHESS *exits the other way as* COOK *throws another pot at her. Curtain.*)

* * *

Scene Five

SETTING: *In the woods.*

AT RISE: CHESHIRE CAT *is sitting in branches of tree at one side of stage.* ALICE *enters, carrying* BABY, *which snorts.*

ALICE: The poor little thing is snorting away like a steam engine! I can hardly hold it. But if I don't take this child away with me, they're sure to kill it in a day or two. (BABY *grunts like a pig.*) Don't grunt! That's not at all a proper way of expressing yourself. (*Looks closely at* BABY) It has a turned-up nose, much more like a snout than a real nose. Also its eyes are very small for a baby's.

BABY (*Snorting*): Oink! Oink!

ALICE: If you are going to turn into a pig, my dear, I'll have nothing more to do with you. Mind now! (BABY *turns into a pig and runs away. See Production Notes.*)

BABY (*Grunting as it exits*): Oink! Oink!

ALICE: If it had grown up, it would have made a dreadfully ugly child; but it makes a rather handsome pig, I think. I've known other children who might do very well as pigs, if one only knew the right way to change them. (ALICE *sees* CHESHIRE CAT *in the tree and walks over to it.*) Cheshire-Puss. Would you tell me, please, which way I ought to go from here?

CHESHIRE CAT: In one direction lives a Hatter. And in the other direction lives a March Hare. Visit either you like: they're both mad.

ALICE: But I don't want to go among mad people.

CHESHIRE CAT: Oh, you can't help that. We're all mad here. Do you play croquet with the Queen today?

ALICE: I should like that very much, but I haven't been invited yet.

CHESHIRE CAT: You'll see me there. By the bye, what became of the baby? I'd nearly forgotten to ask.

ALICE: It turned into a pig.

CHESHIRE CAT: I thought it would. (CAT *disappears.*)

ALICE: I've seen hatters before. The March Hare will be much the most interesting, and perhaps, as this is May, it won't be raving—at least not so much as it was in March.

CHESHIRE CAT (*Reappearing*): Did you say pig or fig?

ALICE: I said *pig!* And I wish you wouldn't keep appearing and vanishing so suddenly. You make me quite giddy.

CHESHIRE CAT: All right! (*He disappears slowly, leaving only his grin. See Production Notes.*)

ALICE: Well! I've often seen a cat without a grin, but a grin without a cat! It's the most curious thing I ever saw in all my life. (ALICE *exits. Curtain.*)

*   *   *

Scene Six

SETTING: *The March Hare's tea party. The March Hare's house is in the background. It has a pair of long ears on its roof. There is a long table at center, with teacups and saucers on it, and a large teapot with its lid off.*

AT RISE: MARCH HARE *and* MAD HATTER *sit at table, arguing and leaning on* DORMOUSE, *who sits between them, sleeping.* ALICE *enters.*

ALICE: Oh, there they are. That must be the March Hare and the Mad Hatter. And look . . . they are resting their elbows on a dormouse. I suppose it doesn't mind.

HATTER *and* MARCH HARE (*Shouting at* ALICE): No room! No room!

ALICE: There's plenty of room.

HATTER: What day of the month is it? (*Holds up his watch*)

ALICE: The fourth.

HATTER: Two days wrong. I told you butter wouldn't suit the works, March Hare.

MARCH HARE: It's the best butter.

HATTER: Yes, but some crumbs must have got in as well. You shouldn't have put it in with the bread knife. (ALICE *looks at watch.*)

ALICE: What a funny watch! It tells the day of the month and doesn't tell what o'clock it is.

HATTER: Why should it? Does your watch tell you what year it is?

ALICE: Of course not. But that's because it stays the same year for such a long time.

HATTER: Which is just the case with mine. We quarreled about it last March, just before *he* went mad, you know. It was at the great concert given by the Queen of Hearts and I had to sing. (HATTER *stands on table and sings, to tune of "Twinkle, Twinkle, Little Star"*)

Twinkle, twinkle, little bat.

How I wonder what you're at.

(*To* ALICE, *speaking*) You've heard the song?

ALICE: Something like it.

HATTER (*Continuing to sing*):

>Up above the world you fly,
>Like a tea-tray in the sky,
>Twinkle, twinkle—

DORMOUSE (*Waking up and singing*): Twinkle, twinkle. . . .

HATTER (*Getting down off table*): Well, I hardly finished the first verse when the Queen bawled out, "He's murdering the time. Off with his head!"

ALICE: How dreadfully savage!

HATTER: And ever since that, he won't do a thing I ask. It's always six o'clock now.

ALICE: Is that the reason so many tea things are put out here?

MARCH HARE: Yes—that's it. It's always tea time and we've no time to wash the cups in between.

ALICE: Then you keep moving 'round, I suppose?

HATTER: Exactly so. As the things get used up. I want a clean cup. Let's all move one place on. (HATTER *and* MARCH HARE *get up and move, carrying* DORMOUSE *with them, and knocking over dishes.*)

ALICE: Ugh! You've spilled the milk jug!

MARCH HARE: Into the teapot with 'im! (MARCH HARE *and* HATTER *lift* DORMOUSE *and try to stuff it into teapot.*)

ALICE: Well, really, now! It's the stupidest tea party I ever was at in all my life! (*She walks away.*) Everything's curious today. I think I may as well go on to the croquet game. (*Exits. Curtain.*)

* * *

Scene Seven

SETTING: *Queen of Hearts's flower gardens.*

AT RISE: CARDS *march onstage and line up against background.* ALICE *enters and looks about.* WHITE RABBIT *enters.*

RABBIT (*Announcing*): Their Royal Majesties, the King and Queen of Hearts! (KING *and* QUEEN OF HEARTS *enter.*)

QUEEN: Off with their heads! Off with their heads! (*Pointing to* ALICE) Who is that girl?

RABBIT: I don't know, Your Majesty.

QUEEN: Idiot! (*To* ALICE) What is your name, child?

ALICE: My name is Alice, so please Your Majesty. (*To herself*) Why, they are only a pack of cards. I needn't be afraid of them.

QUEEN: And why do the rose bushes have white roses? They should be red. Where are the gardeners? Off with their heads!

KING: Their heads are gone, dear.

QUEEN: That's right. (*To* ALICE) Can you play croquet?

ALICE: Yes.

QUEEN: Come then. (*She walks away.*)

ALICE: (*To* WHITE RABBIT): Where's the Duchess?

RABBIT: Sh-h-h! She's under sentence of execution.

ALICE: For what?

RABBIT: She boxed the Queen's ears. (ALICE *laughs softly.*) Hush! The Queen will hear you.

QUEEN: Get to your places! (CARDS *begin to dash about.* QUEEN *continues to bellow.*) Off with their heads! Off with their heads! (*Sounds of* CARDS *muttering are heard.*)

ALICE (*To* RABBIT): They are dreadfully fond of beheading people here.

CHESHIRE CAT (*Appearing*): How do you like the Queen?

ALICE: Not at all. She's so extremely—oh, the Queen is listening—ah . . . likely to win at this game that it's hardly worthwhile playing. (CARDS *continue to scamper about. Muttering sounds increase.*)

QUEEN: Has the Duchess had her head removed?

KING: Let the jury consider their verdict first.

QUEEN: No! No! Sentence first—verdict afterward.

ALICE (*Shouting*): Stuff and nonsense! The idea of having the sentence first!

QUEEN: Hold your tongue!

ALICE: I won't!

QUEEN (*Shouting*): Off with her head!

ALICE: Who cares for you? You're nothing but a pack of cards! (CARDS, KING *and* QUEEN *fly at* ALICE. *She tries to beat them off.* CHESHIRE CAT *disappears and* WHITE RAB-BIT *exits.* ALICE *falls onto the ground and lies as she did in Scene 1. Curtain.*)

*   *   *

Scene Eight

SETTING: *The same as Scene 1.*

AT RISE: ALICE *lies sleeping, in same position as in previous scene.* ALICE'S SISTER *stands nearby, calling to her.*

SISTER: Wake up, Alice dear. Why, what a long sleep you've had.

ALICE (*Waking up and yawning*): Oh! I've had such a curious dream. I must tell you about my strange adventures. There was a rabbit in a waistcoat, and . . .

SISTER: I'm sure it was a curious dream, but now run in to your tea; it's getting late.

ALICE: All right, sister dear. (ALICE *exits.* SISTER *continues to sit.*)

NARRATOR: And so Alice went to tea and her sister sat a long time in the cool grass watching the sun go down. There was a distant rabbit running in the fields—a frightened mouse splashed his way nearby—and she heard the rattle of teacups, half believing she was in Wonderland too. Open her eyes and she would be back to the confused clamor of the busy countryside. But she knew that her little sister, Alice, would always keep the simple and loving heart of childhood and would gather children around her to tell them the strange tale of her dream of Wonderland, remembering her own childhood and the happy summer days. (*Curtain.*)

THE END

Production Notes

ALICE'S ADVENTURES IN WONDERLAND

Number of Puppets: 13 hand puppets, rod puppets, or marionettes, and 4 or more stick puppets for Cards.

Playing Time: 20 minutes.

Description of Puppets: Model the puppets for this show after the original Tenniel illustrations for *Alice's Adventures in Wonderland,* if you like, or design your own puppets and costumes. Use cut-out figures mounted on rods or heavy wire for the Cards. The Dormouse should be a stuffed toy. The baby is a trick puppet with a baby's head on one end of its body, and a pig's head on the other. A dress covers the pig's head, and dress is flipped over to cover baby's head when baby turns into pig. The Cheshire Cat is a cut-out cardboard figure used on the stove in Scene 4. For Scenes 5 and 7, attach the cut-out to the backdrop, behind a sliding panel.

Properties: Book, pots and pans for the Cook (mounted on wires so that you can control them when the Cook "throws" them), pepper shaker and spoon sewn to Cook's hands, and watch, sewn to White Rabbit's hands.

Setting: Use simple sets, with cut-outs on plain black or blue background. Scene 1, A riverbank—a willow tree on a green, grassy knoll. Scene 2, Down by the rabbit hole—a treadmill band of scenery, showing shelves and bookcases. Roll this behind Alice until she falls to the ground. Scene 3, In front of the Duchess's house—a door frame with a working door, and a sign over it reading THE DUCHESS. This scene may be played before the curtain, without scenery, if desired. Scene 4, The Duchess's kitchen

—cut-out of a big, black stove with Cheshire Cat on it. There is a stool center for Duchess. Scene 5, In the woods —a cut-out of a large tree, with a sliding panel in the branches which can be operated from backstage. Behind the panel is the cut-out Cheshire Cat, and on the panel is a drawing of the Cat's "smile"—two rows of teeth arranged in a grin. By sliding the panel you hide the cat and show only the grin. Scene 6, The March Hare's tea party. There is a table center, with six or more chairs arranged behind it. Toy teacups, saucers, and teapot are glued to table. A cut-out of the March Hare's House, with chimneys shaped like long ears, is on the backdrop (this may be omitted). Scene 7, Queen of Hearts's flower garden— background has cut-out rose bushes on it with white roses. Cheshire Cat is on sliding panel in background. Scene 8, Riverbank, as in Scene 1.

Lighting: No special effects.

Sound: Crowd noises, in Scene 7, as indicated in text (use recordings if desired).

THE WIZARD OF OZ

Adapted from the book by L. Frank Baum

Characters

NARRATOR
DOROTHY
TOTO, *her dog*
AUNT EM ⎫
UNCLE HENRY ⎭ *offstage voices*
GOOD WITCH OF THE NORTH
MAYOR OF THE MUNCHKINS
MUNCHKIN LADY
MUNCHKIN BOY
MUNCHKINS
SCARECROW
TIN WOODSMAN
LION
GATE KEEPER
WICKED WITCH OF THE WEST
OZ, *as a dragon*
OZ, *as a large, ugly head*
OZ, *as himself*
CAT

Scene One

SETTING: *Side yard of a little house on the great Kansas prairies. There is a cut-out of side view of house onstage, against a plain background.*
AT RISE: *Stage is empty.*

NARRATOR: Dorothy lived in the midst of the great Kansas prairies, with her Uncle Henry and her Aunt Em. They lived in a one-room house, and not a tree or farm broke the broad sweep of flat country that reached the edge of the sky in all directions.

DOROTHY (*Entering*): Come out, Toto! (TOTO, *her dog, comes out from behind house.*) Let's play ball, Toto. (DOROTHY *holds up ball.*) Come on, Toto—fetch! (*Wailing sound is heard in distance. She throws ball and* TOTO *brings it back.*) Aunt Em! See how Toto plays ball with me! Uncle Henry!

AUNT EM (*From offstage*): Uncle Henry's too tired from working so hard. And I'm doing the dishes, Dorothy.

DOROTHY: Listen, Toto. Hear that strange noise? (*Wailing sound becomes louder*)

TOTO (*Whimpering*): Hmm-hmm-hmm!

UNCLE HENRY (*From offstage*): There's a cyclone coming, Em!

AUNT EM (*From offstage*): Quick, Dorothy! Run for the cellar. (TOTO *runs offstage.*)

DOROTHY: I have to get Toto first. (*She exits after* TOTO.)

UNCLE HENRY (*From offstage*): Come down here, Em!

AUNT EM (*From offstage*): Dorothy! Dorothy! I'm coming, Henry! (*Wind howls furiously. House shakes.* DOROTHY *re-enters with* TOTO.)

DOROTHY: Hurry, Toto. We have to get in the cellar, too.

TOTO (*Barking*): Arf! Arf! Arf! (*They exit behind house just as it is lifted into the sky.*)

DOROTHY (*From offstage, as if in house*): Help! Aunt Em! Uncle Henry! Help me! (*House flies offstage and is quickly exchanged for a smaller model of house which twirls around in mid-air.*)

NARRATOR: Dorothy and Toto didn't get into the cellar in

time. The north and south winds met in the middle of the
cyclone, and the great pressure of the winds on every side
of the house raised it up higher and higher until it was at
the very top of the funnel of air. The cyclone carried
Dorothy miles and miles away from Kansas. (*Curtain*)
After many hours she landed with a kerplunk in the middle of a strange and beautiful countryside.

* * *

Scene Two

SETTING: *The land of the Munchkins, a field with brightly
colored flowers all around. Dorothy's house is onstage,
center. Two bony legs with silver slippers on the feet are
sticking out from under house.*
AT RISE: DOROTHY *enters from house.*

DOROTHY: Toto! It's all right. Come on out. I wonder where
we are? What a pretty place this is. (TOTO *comes out.*)
And look at the little people coming to say hello! (MAYOR,
LADY *and* BOY MUNCHKINS *enter, followed by* GOOD
WITCH OF THE NORTH.)
WITCH OF NORTH (*To* DOROTHY): You are welcome, most
noble sorceress, to the land of the Munchkins.
MAYOR: We are grateful to you for having killed the Wicked
Witch of the East and for setting my people free.
DOROTHY: You are very kind, but there must be some mis-
take. I am only Dorothy, a little girl. I have never killed
anything.
WITCH OF NORTH: Your house did anyway, and that is the
same thing. (*Points to house*) See! There are her two toes
—still sticking out.

DOROTHY: Oh, dear! The house must have fallen on her. Whatever shall we do?

MAYOR: There is nothing to be done. She has held all the Munchkins in bondage for many years, making them slave for her night and day.

LADY: Now we are all set free. Thank you, Dorothy. Come out, little one. (BOY MUNCHKIN *steps forward, holding flowers.*) He's shy.

BOY (*Singing to tune of "Row, Row, Row Your Boat"*):
> Here are flowers for you,
> We're grateful, thanks a lot,
> Keep the flowers fresh and nice,
> Leave them in the pot.

(*Gives flowers to* DOROTHY)

WITCH OF NORTH: Come out, Munchkins. (MUNCHKINS *enter.*)

MUNCHKINS (*Singing to tune of "Row, Row, Row Your Boat"*):
> Thank you very much,
> Won't you be our friend?
> Please, oh please live here with us
> Right in Munchkin land.

DOROTHY: Thank you all very much. (*To* WITCH OF NORTH) Are you a Munchkin too?

WITCH OF NORTH: No, but I am their friend. I am the Witch of the North.

DOROTHY: Oh, gracious! Are you a real witch?

WITCH OF NORTH: Yes, indeed! But I am a *good* witch.

DOROTHY: Can you help me get back home?

WITCH OF NORTH: There is only one who can help you. He is the great Wizard of Oz. He is more powerful than all the rest of us together. He lives in the City of Emeralds.

LADY: Look! (*Points to house*) The Witch of the East is

gone! (*Legs are pulled under house, leaving only silver shoes.*)

MAYOR: There is nothing left of her but her silver shoes!

WITCH OF NORTH: She was so old that she dried up. That is the end of her. Now there is only one truly bad witch still alive, and she lives in the West. (*Taking silver shoes*) The silver shoes are yours, Dorothy. (*Gives shoes to DOROTHY.*)

DOROTHY: Thank you. But I must see the Great Wizard of Oz. How do I find him?

WITCH OF NORTH: You must follow the yellow brick road and continue on it until you come to the gates of the Emerald City of Oz. Here is a kiss. (*She kisses DOROTHY on forehead.*) It will protect you from harm. Goodbye, my dear.

MUNCHKINS (*Together*): Goodbye, Dorothy!

DOROTHY: Goodbye, all my dear little friends. And thank you, Good Witch of the North! (DOROTHY *exits with* TOTO *as all wave goodbye.*)

MUNCHKINS: Goodbye! Goodbye! (*Curtain*)

*   *   *

Scene Three

SETTING: *A cornfield. Stick with Scarecrow on it is at one side.*

AT RISE: DOROTHY *and* TOTO *enter. She carries a basket.*

DOROTHY: Let's rest a while, Toto. We've walked so far and I'm tired. (*She sits down.*)

SCARECROW: Good day!

DOROTHY (*Looking at* SCARECROW): Did you speak?

SCARECROW: I think so. How do you do?

DOROTHY: I'm pretty well, thank you. How do you do?

SCARECROW: I'm not feeling well. It's very tedious being perched up here night and day to scare away the crows . . . and they won't scare. They just laugh at me.

DOROTHY: Can't you get down?

SCARECROW: No—this pole is stuck up my back. If you can, please, get me down. (DOROTHY *takes* SCARECROW *down*.) Thank you very much. I feel like a new man. Where are you going?

DOROTHY: To the Emerald City of Oz, to ask the great Oz to send me back to Kansas.

SCARECROW: Where is the Emerald City—and who is Oz?

DOROTHY: Why, don't you know?

SCARECROW: No, indeed. I don't know anything. You see, I am stuffed, so I have no brains at all.

DOROTHY: Oh, I'm awfully sorry for you.

SCARECROW: Do you think if I go with you that Oz would give me some brains?

DOROTHY: I can't tell, but you may come with me if you like. If Oz will not give you any brains, you will be no worse off than you are now.

SCARECROW: That's true! So off we go.

TOTO (*Growling*): Grr-r-r-r! (SCARECROW *jumps*.)

DOROTHY: Don't mind Toto. He never bites.

SCARECROW: I'm not afraid. He can't hurt the straw. I'll tell you a secret. There is only one thing in the world I'm afraid of and it's a lighted match. Come on—let's go. (*They exit. Curtain.*)

*　　*　　*

Scene Four

SETTING: *A dark forest.*
AT RISE: TIN WOODSMAN *is standing at one side, holding ax in air, not moving.* DOROTHY, TOTO *and* SCARECROW *enter.*

DOROTHY: It's getting dark . . . and the trees are getting thicker.
SCARECROW: If this road goes into the forest, it must come out. And as the Emerald City is at the other end of the road, we must go wherever it leads us.
DOROTHY: Why, anyone would know that!
SCARECROW: Certainly—that is why I know it. If it required brains to figure it out, I never should have said it.
TIN WOODSMAN (*Groaning*): Mmmmm!
DOROTHY: What was that?
SCARECROW: I can't imagine.
TIN WOODSMAN (*Groaning again*): Mmmmm!
DOROTHY (*Seeing* TIN WOODSMAN): Why, it's a man all made of tin. (*To* TIN WOODSMAN) Did you groan?
TIN WOODSMAN: Yes, I did. I've been groaning for more than a year and no one has ever heard me before—or come to help me.
DOROTHY: What can I do for you?
TIN WOODSMAN: Get my oil can and oil my joints. There is one at my feet. (DOROTHY *picks up oil can.*) Oil my neck first. (*She does.*) Now oil the joints of my arms and legs. (*She does. He tries to move legs and arms. Squeaking sounds are heard. He lowers arms.*) Ah-h-h! That feels good. This is a great comfort. I have been holding that ax in the air ever since I rusted. I'm glad to be able to put it down at last! I am very grateful to you.
DOROTHY: Oh, that's all right.

TIN WOODSMAN: I might have stood there always if you hadn't come along. So you have certainly saved my life. How did you happen to be here?

DOROTHY: We are on our way to the Emerald City to see the great Oz.

TIN WOODSMAN: Why do you wish to see Oz?

DOROTHY: I want him to send me back to Kansas, and the Scarecrow wants him to put a few brains into his head.

TIN WOODSMAN: Do you suppose Oz could give me a heart?

DOROTHY: Why, I guess so. It would be as easy as giving the Scarecrow brains.

SCARECROW: Come along!

DOROTHY: We would be pleased to have your company.

TIN WOODSMAN: All right. Off we go! And bring my oil can, too. (DOROTHY *puts oil can into basket and all four start to move off together. Suddenly* TOTO *begins to bark.*)

TOTO (*Loudly*): Arf! Arf! Arf!

DOROTHY: What is it, Toto?

LION (*From offstage, roaring loudly*): Gr-r-r! (LION *comes bounding in.*) Gr-r-r! (LION *sends* SCARECROW *and* TIN WOODSMAN *sprawling.* DOROTHY *screams.* LION *starts for* TOTO, *who is still barking.* DOROTHY, *furious, hits* LION *on nose. He suddenly begins to whimper and cry.*)

DOROTHY: Don't you dare to bite Toto! You ought to be ashamed of yourself. A big beast like you—biting a poor little dog.

LION (*Still crying*): I didn't bite him.

DOROTHY: No—but you tried to. You are nothing but a big coward.

LION: I know it. I've always known it. But how can I help it?

DOROTHY: I don't know, I'm sure. To think of you striking a stuffed man like the poor scarecrow!

LION: Is he stuffed?

DOROTHY: Of course he's stuffed. (DOROTHY *picks up* SCARE-CROW.)

LION: Is the other one stuffed also?

DOROTHY: No. He's made of tin.

LION: That's why he nearly blunted my claws. What is that little animal made of? Straw or tin?

DOROTHY: Neither. He's a—a—a meat dog.

LION: Now that I look at him, no one would think of biting such a little thing except a coward like me.

DOROTHY: What makes you a coward?

LION: It's a mystery to me, but I've learned that if I roar very loudly, every living thing is frightened and gets out of my way.

SCARECROW: But that isn't right. The King of the Beasts shouldn't be a coward.

LION: I know it. (*Sobs*) It is my great sorrow and makes my life very unhappy. But whenever there is danger, my heart begins to beat fast.

TIN WOODSMAN: Perhaps you have heart trouble.

LION: It may be.

SCARECROW: I am going to the great Oz to ask him to give me some brains.

TIN WOODSMAN: And I am going to ask him to give me a heart.

DOROTHY: And I am going to ask him to send Toto and me back to Kansas.

LION: Do you think Oz could give me courage?

DOROTHY: Perhaps he can.

LION: Then, if you don't mind, I'll go with you.

DOROTHY: You are very welcome. (*They start off together. Curtain.*)

* * *

Scene Five

SETTING: *The gates of the Emerald City of Oz.*
AT RISE: DOROTHY, TOTO, LION, SCARECROW *and* TIN
WOODSMAN *enter.*

DOROTHY: Look! That must be the Emerald City of Oz.
SCARECROW: I'll push this button and see if someone will let
us in. (*He touches gate.*)
GATE KEEPER (*Entering*): What do you want in the Emer-
ald City of Oz?
DOROTHY: We wish to see the great Oz.
GATE KEEPER: It has been many years since anyone asked to
see Oz. He is powerful and terrible, and if you come on an
idle or foolish errand to bother his wise reflections, he
might be angry and destroy you all in an instant.
SCARECROW: But it is not a foolish errand, nor an idle one.
It is important. We have been told that Oz is a good
Wizard.
GATE KEEPER: Yes, he is . . . and he rules the Emerald City
wisely and well. But to those who are not honest, or who
approach him from curiosity, he is most terrible. However,
since you have asked to see the great Oz, I must take you
to his palace. Come in! (*They all cross and exit. Curtain.*)

*   *   *

Scene Six

SETTING: *Oz's throne room. There is a throne at center. At
one side is a curtained booth.*
AT RISE: OZ, *in the form of a dragon, is sitting on throne.*

DOROTHY, TOTO, LION, TIN WOODSMAN, *and* SCARECROW *enter.*

OZ: I am Oz, the great and terrible. Who are you and why do you seek me?

DOROTHY: I am Dorothy, the small and meek. This is the Scarecrow, the Tin Woodsman, the Cowardly Lion, and my dog, Toto. We have come for your help.

OZ: Where did you get those silver shoes?

DOROTHY: I got them from the Wicked Witch of the East when my house fell on her and killed her.

OZ: And where did you get that mark upon your forehead?

DOROTHY: That is where the Good Witch of the North kissed me when she sent me to you.

OZ: What do you wish me to do?

SCARECROW: Please, I would like to have some brains.

TIN WOODSMAN: And I would passionately like to have a heart.

LION: And I would like to have courage.

OZ: And you, girl?

DOROTHY: Please send me back to Kansas and my Aunt Em and Uncle Henry.

OZ: Why should I do this for you?

DOROTHY: Because you are strong and we are weak; and because you are a great Wizard and we are helpless.

OZ: You have no right to expect me to do these things unless you will do something for me in return. In this country everyone must pay for everything he gets.

SCARECROW: What must we do?

OZ: Kill the Wicked Witch of the West. She is the only wicked witch left in all this land.

TIN WOODSMAN: But we cannot!

Oz: The girl killed the Witch of the East, and now she wears the silver shoes which bear a powerful charm. When you can tell me the Wicked Witch of the West is dead, I will do all you ask of me . . . but not before. Now—go! (DOROTHY, TOTO, SCARECROW, TIN WOODSMAN *and* COWARDLY LION *exit, leaving* Oz *on throne. Curtain.*)

*　　*　　*

Scene Seven

SETTING: *The red castle of the Wicked Witch of the West.*
AT RISE: DOROTHY, TOTO, SCARECROW, LION *and* TIN WOODSMAN *enter.*

LION: I don't know why we came. This is such a spooky place. Maybe we had better go back and tell Oz we won't do it.
TIN WOODSMAN: Don't be such a scaredy-cat. Everything will be all—(WICKED WITCH OF THE WEST *enters, carrying a torch.*)
WITCH OF WEST: So. . . . You have come to visit me, have you? You have escaped my slaves, have you? The Tin Woodsman killed my wolves, the Scarecrow destroyed my crows and the Lion scared away my Winkies . . . but my winged monkeys brought you here to me. Now I will get rid of you myself.
SCARECROW: Don't you dare touch any of us, you ugly Witch of the West. Dorothy is protected by the kiss of the Good Witch of the North.
WITCH OF WEST: Ah, yes. The little girl. (*To* DOROTHY) How did you get those silver shoes? Give them to me.

DOROTHY: But the Witch of the North said they were mine now.

WITCH OF WEST: Give them to me, I say! (*She starts for* DOROTHY.)

LION (*Roaring*): Gr-r-r-r-r! Don't go near Dorothy or I'll bite you.

WITCH OF WEST: Ah! A spirited lion. Good! You will be my slave and draw my black carriage.

LION: Never!

WITCH OF WEST: Tin Woodsman, you can build me a new castle with your ax.

TIN WOODSMAN: I'll use this ax on you!

WITCH OF WEST: Scarecrow, you would make a nice little fire! (*She starts toward* SCARECROW *with her torch.*)

SCARECROW: No! No! Stay away. I'm afraid of fire. Stay away!

WITCH OF WEST: He-he-heee! Just a little taste, my straw friend. He-he-heee!

DOROTHY: You leave my friends alone, you ugly, bad Witch! (DOROTHY *picks up a bucket of water.*)

WITCH OF WEST (*Frightened*): What are you going to do with that water? Put it down! Put it down!

DOROTHY: You stay away from the Scarecrow! (DOROTHY *throws the water on* WITCH. *A loud hissing sound is heard.* WITCH *begins to melt.*)

WITCH OF WEST (*Shrieking*): Ah-h-h-h! See what you have done? In a minute I shall melt away!

DOROTHY: I'm very sorry!

WITCH OF WEST: Didn't you know water would be the end of me?

DOROTHY: Of course not. How could I have known?

WITCH OF WEST: Well, in a few minutes I shall be all melted

and you will have this castle to yourself. I never thought a little girl like you would end my wicked deeds. Look out —here I go. . . . (WITCH *disappears. Only her hat is left.*)

ALL: Hurray! The Wicked Witch of the West is dead!

SCARECROW: Quickly! Back to the Wizard of Oz. (*All rush out as curtains close.*)

*   *   *

Scene Eight

SETTING: *The same as Scene 6.*

AT RISE: OZ, *in the form of a large, ugly head, is sitting on throne.* DOROTHY, TOTO, SCARECROW, TIN WOODSMAN, *and* LION *enter.*

OZ: What? You have returned already? Go away and come back tomorrow. I need time to think over your requests.

TIN WOODSMAN: You've had plenty of time already.

SCARECROW: We won't wait a day longer.

DOROTHY: You must keep your promises to us. (LION *roars.*)

LION: Give me my courage—*now!*

TOTO (*Barking*): Arf! Arf! Arf! (TOTO *runs over to booth and pulls open curtain revealing* WIZARD OF OZ, *a short, kind-looking man, standing at a control panel.*)

TIN WOODSMAN: Who are you?

OZ (*Meekly*): I am Oz, the great and terrible, but please don't strike me. Please don't! I'll do anything you want me to.

DOROTHY: What? Aren't you a great wizard?

OZ: Hush, my dear. Don't speak so loudly or you'll be overheard—and I shall be ruined. I'm supposed to be a great wizard!

DOROTHY: And aren't you?

OZ: I'm afraid not, my dear. I'm just a common man.

SCARECROW: You're more than that. You're a humbug!

OZ (*Pleased*): Exactly so. I am a humbug.

LION: But what about the things you promised us?

OZ: I have them right here. (*Takes diploma from control booth and hands it to* SCARECROW.) Scarecrow, here is a diploma, to prove that you have brains.

SCARECROW (*Taking diploma*): Thank you. I feel brilliant already.

OZ (*Taking small heart from control booth*): Tin Woodsman, here is your heart—but I think you are wrong to want it. It makes most people unhappy. (*Places heart on* TIN WOODSMAN'*s chest*)

TIN WOODSMAN: Thank you. I shall never forget your kindness. (OZ *takes bottle from control booth and gives it to* LION.)

OZ: Lion, drink this little bottle of courage. (LION *drinks, making gulping sounds.*)

LION: Oh, that's delicious! It tastes like cinnamon cider. Thank you very much.

DOROTHY: What about me?

OZ: I think I have found a way to get us both back to Kansas, Dorothy. Tomorrow you and I will sail away in a large balloon—back to Kansas.

DOROTHY: Oh, thank you! (*Curtain.*)

*   *   *

Scene Nine

SETTING: *The same as Scene 5.*

AT RISE: *There is a large balloon with a basket hanging below it at center. Oz is in the basket. DOROTHY and TOTO are on the ground, talking to SCARECROW, TIN WOODSMAN, and LION.*

OZ: Hurry, Dorothy! Get into the basket. Hurry, or the balloon will fly away without you.

DOROTHY: Goodbye, my friends. I will miss you all very much.

OZ: Goodbye, everyone. Hurry, Dorothy! (CAT *suddenly runs onstage.* TOTO *barks and begins to chase it.* DOROTHY *chases* TOTO. *Balloon starts to float into the air.*)

DOROTHY (*To* OZ): Come back! I want to go too! (*Balloon rises.*)

OZ: I can't come back, my dear. Goodbye! (*He sails out of sight in balloon.* CAT *exits and* TOTO *returns to* DOROTHY's *side.*)

DOROTHY: Oh, no! (*She begins to cry.*) What shall I do? I'll never get back to Kansas now! (*Weeps.*)

SCARECROW: Don't cry, Dorothy.

TIN WOODSMAN: You are making me cry, too. (*Sniffs*) I must have a heart, for it is making me very unhappy now.

LION: Poor Dorothy! (WITCH OF NORTH *enters.*)

WITCH OF NORTH: Dorothy, your silver shoes will carry you home, whenever you want to go. They can carry you any place in the world, in three steps. All you have to do is knock the heels together three times, and command them to take you home.

DOROTHY: Then I shall return home at once. Goodbye, all my wonderful friends.

ALL: Goodbye, Dorothy.

DOROTHY: I love you all and shall never forget you.

ALL: Goodbye. (*She picks up* TOTO. *He barks.*)

DOROTHY: Silver shoes, take me home to Aunt Em. (*She clicks heels of shoes together three times, and flies offstage with* TOTO *as all wave. Curtain.*)

*   *   *

Scene Ten

SETTING: *Kansas. This scene is played in front of curtain.*

BEFORE CURTAIN: DOROTHY *and* TOTO *enter.*

DOROTHY: Aunt Em! Uncle Henry! I'm home. I'm back home again! (DOROTHY *and* TOTO *cross stage and exit.*)

THE END

Production Notes

THE WIZARD OF OZ

Number of Puppets: 13 hand puppets, marionettes, or rod puppets, or any combination of these, plus cut-outs for as many Munchkins as desired, cut-out of Oz as dragon, and cut-out of Oz as large, ugly head.

Playing Time: 20 minutes.

Description of Puppets: Use imagination in designing these puppets. Dorothy is a little girl with a simple dress. If her feet are visible, she wears silver shoes from Scene 3 on. She has a basket over her arm from Scene 3 on. Good Witch of the North and Wicked Witch of West are dressed alike, in long gowns, but Good Witch has a white gown and Wicked Witch a black gown. Wicked Witch wears a peaked black hat. If the Wicked Witch is a marionette, make a head and hands attached to a full, loose costume, so that when she melts, the costume sinks to the floor and her head goes into her hat. Tin Woodsman may be made of a series of tin cans, or cardboard rolls painted silver. Scarecrow is in patched shirt and pants, with straw sticking out of clothing. He wears a floppy hat. Lion is in an appropriate animal costume. Toto and Cat are loosely stuffed animal toys. A removable rod should be attached to Toto so that he can be in Dorothy's basket during Scenes 5, 6, and 7. Munchkins are short, cute little people in bright, colorful clothes.

Properties: Ball for Dorothy and Toto in Scene 1 (put it on a wire so that it can be controlled from backstage); pair of legs with silver shoes on them; bouquet of flowers; oil can; torch (red foil on a stick) sewn to hand of Wicked Witch;

167

diploma; heart (put tape or a pin on back of heart so that it will stick to Tin Woodsman's body); bottle; bucket containing shredded cellophane for "water"; cut-out of balloon with basket hanging below it; small, three-dimensional model of Dorothy's house, on a heavy wire or dowel, for Scene 1.

Setting: There are seven basic settings: Scene 1, Dorothy's house in Kansas—there is a cut-out of the house, side view, onstage. The background is plain. Scene 2, the land of the Munchkins—background shows a field with flowers growing all about. Scene 3, cornfield—background is plain and a cut-out or drawing of a fence is on it. There is a stick for Scarecrow at one side. Scene 4, forest—background shows dark, gnarled trees, cut-outs or painted on backdrop. Scenes 5 and 9, gates of the Emerald City of Oz—impressive, large green gates are painted on backdrop. Scenes 6 and 8, throne room—green draperies at rear, throne center, and small booth with curtain across it at one side. Curtain should be hung on rings so that it can be easily slid back—tie a string to it and pull curtain aside from backstage when Toto tugs at curtain. Suggestion of dials, knobs, levers, etc., should be drawn on control panel inside booth. Scene 7, red castle of Wicked Witch—painting on backdrop of red, forbidding castle with stone arches, turrets, spikes and chains hanging from walls, etc.

Lighting: No special effects.

Sound: Whining sound of wind for cyclone; squeaking sound for Tin Woodsman; hissing sound for Wicked Witch when water hits her; all as indicated in text.

HOW TO PRODUCE A PUPPET SHOW

HOW TO PRODUCE A PUPPET SHOW

The following pages are meant to help you produce the twelve plays in this book. Although there have been many "how-to" books on puppet construction and the production of a puppet show, the following is meant to show you the easy way for beginners and the young.

Most of the plays can be done as hand puppet, rod puppet, or marionette shows. Produce the play as you see fit, and would enjoy doing it. A lot depends on the time you have to produce the show—hand puppets take less time than marionettes, for example. Some stories lend themselves better to one kind of puppet than another, also.

Puppet plays are lots of fun to do and see, and you can learn much about theater and how to get along with each other through this wonderful world of puppets.

Designs for Simple Puppets

Here are some ideas for easy puppets that would be fun to make. They can be made in a short time from household utensils, wooden spoons, handkerchiefs, fly swatters, flip-top cigarette boxes, milk cartons, cracker or cereal boxes, paper bags, paper cups, gloves, crepe paper, cardboard, old toys,

Designs for simple puppets: A. Fly swatter puppet; B. Milk carton puppet with handkerchief blanket; C. Paper bag puppet; D. Cereal box puppet with cloth tube neck; E. Paper doll puppet backed with cardboard and with paper fasteners at leg and arm joints, mounted on a rod or string; F. Flip-top cigarette box puppet with rubber band at jaw, and mounted on stick; G. Paper sculpture puppet on a stick; H. Glove puppet with furry ball and eyes; I. Finger puppet; J. Wooden spoon puppet with cloth skirt.

vegetables, and similar materials. See if you can find some interesting objects around the house and make puppets out of them.

Making Papier-Mâché *Puppet Heads*

Paper-covered puppet heads are inexpensive and easy to make. There are three types of bases on which you can build your *papier-mâché* puppet heads: a styrofoam ball; a crumpled newspaper ball; an inflated balloon. Before applying paste and paper to the styrofoam or newspaper balls, put a cardboard tube (from wax paper, paper towels, etc.) into the center for a neck. (Put the tube into the balloon head after *papier-mâché* is dry and break the balloon.) Be sure your index finger fits the tube. Tear newspaper into small pieces, apply flour-and-water paste or school paste to each piece and apply them to the puppet head until the head is covered with three or four layers of the torn paper. Be sure to bring the paper strips down onto the tube for strength. Next add the nose, ears, brows, eyes, and chin with more paper.

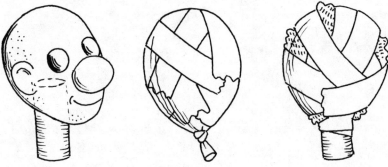

Papier-mâché puppet heads.

There is a commercial pulp *papier-mâché* called "Papier-Mâché Clay" that you can buy in most craft, art or hobby shops. You add only water because the adhesive is already in it. Apply this directly to a styrofoam ball, but for newspaper balls or balloons, apply a layer of torn paper strips and paste before applying the Clay. It is very good for facial features, because it molds easily, like putty or modeling clay. Be careful to apply a *thin* coat of Papier-Mâché Clay so that it dries quickly and doesn't crack. Use poster paints or acrylics to paint the head.

If you are making a marionette head, put heavy wire loops on each side of the head for strings. Also, glue a short dowel into the neck tube and put a screw eye in the exposed end of the dowel so that the body can be attached to the head.

Yarn, cord, or unraveled rope makes good hair. You can also use construction paper cut into fringe, felt, or a steel-wool pad for a wig. Save corks, buttons and beads to use for eyes and noses.

Simple Hand Puppets

There are two kinds of simple hand puppet body patterns you can try. Use soft fabrics such as muslin or cotton so that the puppet moves easily. It would be wise to make a simple sketch of the costume first.

The shaped hand puppet body: Cut two pieces of fabric in the shape shown in the drawing. Note that the front piece is narrower than the back. The front piece is approximately 4″ across at the waist. The back is approximately 5″ across at the waist. Sew these two pieces together, leaving the neck and the bottom open. Then glue the neck tube of the puppet head into the neck opening of the puppet body. Cut felt hands and fit them over the ends of the arms on the puppet body.

The shaped hand puppet body.

The flat hand puppet body, with head.

If you wish, you can make the puppet body out of muslin, attach the hands and head to this, and then dress the hand puppet over the muslin. You can add capes, aprons, collars, belts, ribbons, buttons, or any other trim to complete the costume.

The flat hand puppet body, with head: Cut two pieces of a heavy fabric, such as felt, in the shape shown in the drawing. Note that the head is part of the body pattern and that the two pieces are the same size. Sew the two pieces together, leaving the bottom open. Stuff the head with cotton batting, then decorate the puppet with felt trim, buttons, costume jewelry, etc. This simple puppet pattern is excellent for making animals like cats, owls, dogs, mice, etc. People puppets may also be constructed in this fashion.

Fundamentals of Hand Puppet Manipulation

There are two ways to place your hand inside a hand puppet, both illustrated here:

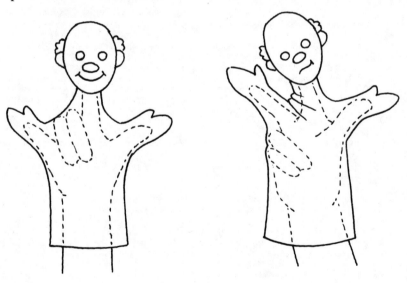

In the first, which is our choice, place your index (pointing) finger in the puppet's head, and your thumb and little finger in the hands of the puppet. This way the figure stands straight and does not look out of shape, nor does it lean. It is more comfortable, and the second and third fingers fill out the chest, so the puppet seems more erect.

The second method is the old European hand puppet position. Perhaps this method is best for you if your little finger is small and you do not have good control of it. Put your index finger in the puppet's head, and your thumb and second finger in his hands. Comfort is the most important consideration in deciding which method to use.

Basic movements

Standing: Hold the puppet erect with your thumb and little finger crooked. Try to hold the puppet's hands out in front of it, but with the hands facing forward.

Bowing: Bend from your wrist, which is your puppet's waist. *Never* bend the whole puppet forward from your elbow—it will look as if it is falling forward with its legs straight. Remember this when the puppet picks up a prop.

Nodding: Bend the first two joints of your index finger.

Turning head from side to side: Either turn the entire body to the side, or else place the upstage puppet hand against the cheek and turn the head with your finger. You can also make the head tube wide enough for two fingers, and the tube long enough inside the costume for the second finger to twist.

Clapping: Close your thumb and little finger together, and return to the spread hand position. *Never* crumple your fingers together to "crush in" the puppet's body. Always think "full chest."

Walking: Use a soft up-and-down motion as you move the

puppet along to convey walking. There are many other rhythms and motions you can try, too, depending upon the age, mood and kind of character your puppet is portraying.

Running: Lean your puppet forward a bit as you quickly move it up and down and forward. This motion, like walking, varies with the kind of puppet it is.

In general, remember that your hand is the whole body of the puppet and not just an extension of your own body movements. Try to show crying, laughing, being angry, and all the other emotions and body movements you can think of. In a rehearsal, think through the action required, and block the broad movements for a scene first. Then smooth out the little movements and reactions to what is being said. Keep the action going. And, above all, practice—practice—*practice!*

The Sock Puppet

The sock puppet is a favorite with children because its mouth moves. You can buy new socks to make it, but well-worn soft socks do just as well. Make a cut in the toe of the sock about 3" deep, as shown, and turn the sock inside out. Cut out a felt mouthpiece in the shape of a large oval, sew a tongue to this if desired (see drawing), and pin the felt oval into the opening in the cut sock. Sew in place by hand or machine, stitching felt teeth into place at the same time if desired, then turn the sock right side out. Now sew eyes, brows, ears, scales, etc., onto the sock. Felt or any other heavy material may be used for this. Shiny buttons or fake jewels may be used for eyes.

Instead of a sock, you can also use a tube of fake fur, wool felt, or jersey, following the method described above. Experiment to make wonderful, imaginative animals or monsters.

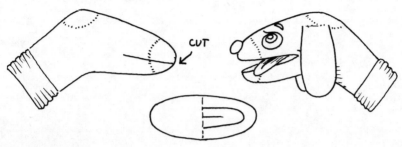

The sock puppet.

When the puppet is finished, put your hand in it and try talking at the same time as you move its mouth. Can you lip sync—that is, move the puppet's mouth to fit your words? Work at it. You'll be surprised how much fun it can be.

The Rag Doll Marionette

If you like to sew, you may enjoy making a rag doll marionette for your performance. Follow the simple design on page 180. The body, legs, and feet are cut in one piece, and the arms and head are separate. Either make a *papier-mâché* head as previously described, or make a stuffed rag doll head, following the drawing.

Sew the back and front pieces of the body section together, turn right side out, and fill the feet with sand. Make two rows of stitches across the ankles, then stuff with cotton to the knees. Make another double row of stitches, stuff to the hips, and make two more rows of stitching. Stuff the body and sew the shoulders closed by hand. Sew and reverse the arm and hand pieces. Stuff the hands with sand and make a double row of stitches at the wrists. Stuff to the elbows with cotton, and stitch twice. Stuff just a bit to fill out the upper arm and attach it to the shoulder of the body section. If you

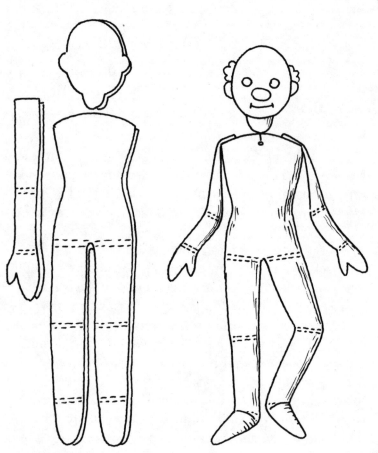

The rag doll marionette.

are using a stuffed head, sew, reverse, and stuff, then attach to the center of the shoulder area.

Paint the face and hands. Then attach the wig and dress your marionette. To complete the feet, sew them at right angles to the ankles, and either paint shoes on them, or cover with felt.

The Marionette Control and How to Use It

When your marionette is completed, the next step is to make a marionette control and string the marionette. The marionette control consists of three wooden sticks. Molding strips ½″ × ¾″ are ideal, though you can use laths as well. The main bar with which you hold the control is 9″ long. The shortest bar is 5″ long and is for the head strings. Nail this to the main bar about three inches from the front (see drawing on page 182). The third bar is 7″ long. It is for the leg strings, and must be detachable in order to "walk" the marionette. Drill a hole in the middle of the bar, and put a nail or peg in the front of the main bar to hold the third bar when it is not in use.

Attach black, dark blue, or gray carpet thread to the marionette on each side of its head, on each shoulder, on each knee, on each wrist, and on the back. If you use a *papier-mâché* puppet head, you will probably need to insert a loop of heavy wire on each side of the head above the ears. For cloth heads, sew strings directly on each side above the ears. The strings should be at least 2′ long, or longer, if your backdrops are high. Attach the strings to the control with staples, or else tie the strings to the control bars and glue in place. Always start with the head strings and hang the marionette during the rest of the stringing.

Try working your marionette. Hold it standing erect with its feet just touching the floor. Bend the control forward for

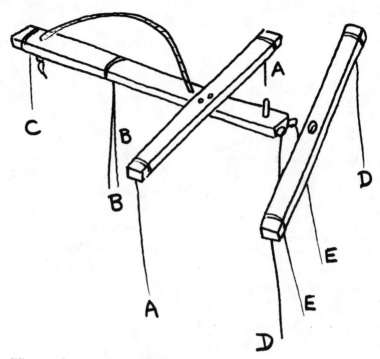

The marionette control, showing strings: A—the head strings; B—the shoulder strings; C—the back string; D—the knee strings; E—the hand strings.

bowing. Try sitting the marionette down on a low box, or on your foot. Keep its knees up. Try working its hands. Now use your other hand to take the leg bar off its peg and try walking the marionette. It's tricky, but with practice, you'll succeed. Bob the marionette up and down ever so slightly as you tilt its leg bar from side to side while moving the whole control forward. Turn the marionette's head from side to side by bending it forward, taking the weight off the head strings, and then turning the main bar from side to side.

The marionette with strings attached.

Simple Puppet Stages

Here are a few easy stages for hand puppets and marionettes. The most common stage is one with the proscenium opening. You can make it from a large cardboard refrigerator or television carton. A wooden frame covered with muslin or cardboard will hold up better under heavy use, however. The drawing below illustrates this kind of theater for hand puppets or marionettes. When you do a marionette show just turn the stage over, stand behind it and work over the scenery support.

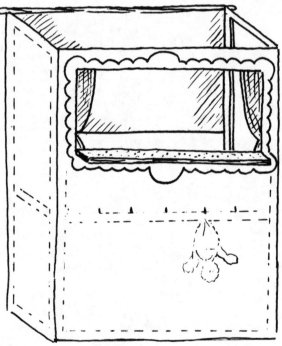

Cardboard or wood frame puppet theater.

To construct the theater, make three rectangles of wood strips as in the drawing, glue muslin or cardboard to each wooden frame, and paint. Cut out the proscenium opening, and hang a curtain rod and curtains to cover the opening, if you wish. Also hang a light background curtain at back.

Another important feature of this stage is the "playboard" or apron. This is a board about 4″ wide across the bottom of the proscenium on which props and puppet furniture can be placed. The playboard is not necessary for marionette shows, when the stage is turned upside down.

Another type of puppet theater is the "open proscenium" hand puppet stage (below) that is excellent for plays requir-

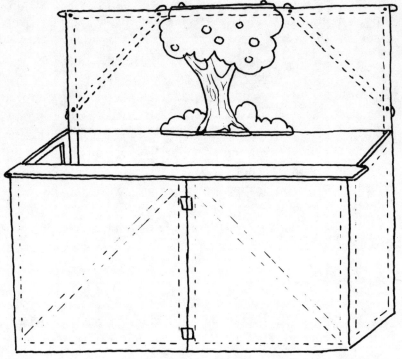

"Open proscenium" hand or rod puppet stage.

ing a large number of puppeteers. With this type of stage, there is an unlimited view of the action (the closed proscenium theater does have limited sight lines). Set pieces and scenery are hung from the back support and placed on the playboard. The bottom section is in four pieces, built like the stage above, and it should be hinged so that it can be folded when not in use. This stage front should be high enough to hide the tallest puppeteer and low enough to enable the littlest puppeteer to hold his puppet in view.

To make a quick puppet stage: Fasten a blanket or sheet to a stick, and have two children hold the ends of the stick up; put a tension curtain rod in a doorway and hang a curtain from it—use the open area above it for your proscenium opening; get a large cardboard box or packing crate, cut the top off it, and have the puppeteers stand inside and play over the top of the box.

Props for the Puppet Stage

Props and scenery can be as much fun to make as puppets themselves. Save boxes of many sizes to make such props as chairs, couches, thrones, chests, tables and cabinets. Easter baskets, Halloween noisemakers, and other toys make good small hand props. Shrubbery and trees can be cut from cardboard, painted and propped up on a stand. You can also make interesting greenery from crushed newspaper, and flowers from tissue or construction paper. Old sponges are good for making bushes, too. Real branches are always intriguing to the eye.

Scenery

You can paint backdrops on brown wrapping paper, butcher paper, or muslin, but to simplify the stage design, use a set piece—a single piece of scenery, such as a tree or house front cut out of cardboard, which leaves the rest of the stage free for easy action. For example, a throne room would have just one large impressive throne—and a banner or two to add color. A whole forest can be suggested with one large tree and a dark background or green cloth. Change the background to a light color, and you have a garden. Even a fence with flowers on it tells the audience it is a friendly outdoor place. Perhaps your play may call for no scenery at all if it is short and the puppets are delightful to look at.

Materials and Supplies and Where to Get Them

Felt is good for making puppet heads, hands and other parts of the puppet body. You can also use it for hats, vests, shoes, and just about any part of the costumes or trim. Use the half-wool, half-synthetic blend of felt. It's cheaper and easier to work with. Felt usually comes 72″ wide in a very large range of colors, including four or five flesh tones from light pink or champagne to beige or tan. Small felt squares are also excellent when you need only a small quantity of one color. Felt is available at department stores, variety shops, craft and art supply stores and dime stores.

Yarn, embroidery floss, raffia and burlap all make good puppet hair. Cotton rug yarn is cheap and goes a long way. Other wool yarns are good, too, but more expensive. Stores mentioned above usually carry these products too.

Wood can be used for many things in puppetry. A soft, good grade of pine is best for almost everything you might want to build or carve. Local lumber yards carry it in just the width and thickness you need. Plywood is excellent for thin, strong joints. Never use balsa wood, however—it is seldom strong enough.

Styrofoam is good for many things. It comes in ¼″ to 2″ thicknesses, and in various ball and egg shapes. Although it may be a bit expensive, it is very light, easy to handle, and cuts down your work. You can buy it at craft or hobby stores, flower supply houses, decorator and display houses, and the dime stores.

Paint is an important material in puppetry. Buy a good grade of latex white house paint. Mix cheap liquid or powder temperas (poster paints) into small amounts of the latex white paint for puppet heads, scenery, props, costumes and just about everything. It can be scrubbed when dirty and dries fast; it is opaque and doesn't crack if it is not put on too thickly. All paint stores carry the latex household paints.

Costume fabrics should be light-weight for easy movement of the puppet. The best fabrics are jerseys, cottons, light velvets, silks, satins and soft, rough-textured materials. If necessary, wash the fabric before cutting it to make the material softer. Keep your patterns small and in scale to the puppet. Yard goods shops, department stores, and dime stores carry many of the fabrics you can use.

Scenery fabric can be inexpensive unbleached muslin, which comes in various widths and paints well. Use this for backdrops, covering frames, and making scenery and props.

Charcoal pencils are excellent for sketching in your scenery before painting. They are easier to see than ordinary pencil and not so messy as chalk. You can buy them at your local art or craft supplies dealer. School supply houses may carry them, too.

Black light and black-light paints are luminous products which are fun to use for special effects when you want things to glow in the dark. If you have a costume supply house in your town, it will probably carry these products, or write Shannon Luminous Materials Co., 7356 Santa Monica Blvd., Los Angeles, Calif. 90046.

Papier-mâché clay is a paper pulp with glue already in it.

It comes in a powdery form, and all you add is water to get a putty-like working material. It's great for forming features on puppet heads, hands or feet, hats, and many other puppet items. The thinner it is, the faster it dries. If it is used thick, it is probably best to dry it in a warm oven to take out the moisture. There are a number of brands of varying qualities, but the best is "Celluclay" because of its smooth texture. Most art and craft or hobby shops carry this product.

"*Sculpey*" is a modeling plastic that stays soft indefinitely or bakes hard in fifteen minutes in your oven. Polyform Products (9420 Bryon St., Schiller Park, Ill. 60176) is the firm that makes it, but it may be found in art, hobby or craft shops. This material is also good for molding features on puppet heads.

How to Get the Most Out of Your Rehearsals

You can't just make a set of puppets, wiggle them in front of an audience, and expect your play to be a success. A good production is like a chain—each link is important to make a good show. Let's assume you have the following: (1) a good puppet script or storyline; (2) puppets that look good from a distance and work easily and well; (3) scenery or set pieces that look good from a distance and carry out the mood of your show; (4) lights that give your show good visibility and create the proper mood; (5) sufficient practice in working a puppet. Now you're ready to start your rehearsals. Here are a few simple rules to follow to get the most out of them:

I. The director should (a) listen to the recorded tape of the show or know the script well if the dialogue is to be live; (b) plot the action so he knows who is going where and when; (c) understand about the particular movements of the characters—i.e., an old man moves slowly, a child skips along, etc.; (d) figure out any dances the puppets might have to do; and (e) think about the action of the curtains, lights and scenery.

II. With the puppeteers (a) sit down and listen to the recorded tape with the scripts. If the show is to be live, the puppeteers should memorize their lines and be able to speak their parts without the scripts; (b) decide which puppeteers should do what parts. Also include all curtain pulling and scenery changing as part of the action of the puppeteers. Sometimes non-puppeteers can be assigned to do these specific jobs; (c) have the puppeteers try the puppets or marionettes they are to use, and check the following—(1) are the marionettes' strings long enough when they lie down? (2) do the puppeteers understand the marionette controls? (3) are the hand puppets large enough and do the hand puppets' hands fit the fingers of the operator for easy hand movement?

III. Have the puppeteers "walk through" the show with the puppets to get a general idea of pace (how fast the show moves). First, try it without the recorded tape of speeches, then with it. Next, for each scene, carefully figure out the action and blocking, that is, the arranging of characters on stage for importance of character and good spacing and grouping. Be sure to *use the whole stage.* Use the back area as well as the front of your stage. If there are to be any dances, set them aside until the whole action of the play has been thought out, and then go back and rehearse them.

IV. Assemble the show. Put all the separate parts of rehearsals together, and rehearse, rehearse, and *rehearse again!* Remember, the movement of the scenery and curtains is an essential part of the show, too. Don't have dead spaces of time when nothing is happening onstage. Keep the time between scenes very short. Your scene changes should not take more than thirty seconds. You can also change scenery in front of the audience—this gives them something to look at and can on occasion provide more action than the puppets themselves in the course of the play. If necessary, rehearse with the few puppeteers that need more practice, or with those that are doing the longer parts. Those not rehearsing can be working on scenery or props.

V. The dress rehearsal is really like a first performance. All the puppets, scenery, props and lights should be assembled and tested to see if they are all in good working order. Then go straight through the show without stopping. Perhaps you can have some friends in the audience to tell you what seems wrong or doesn't look right to them. Take their criticisms seriously. You can't think of everything! Remember, they are there to enjoy the show and to help you.

Always cooperate with each other backstage. Puppeteers are usually anxious to please, and have come to enjoy themselves. Try not to lose your temper. Usually you will know who is the best puppeteer for the most important part. Where possible, share equally all the good roles, and remember that *the show is the thing.* As the director, listen to what others have to say, and then use your own good judgment. You have the final say! Stress that the puppeteers must keep cool. If you or anyone else makes a mistake during a performance, *do not panic!* Try to keep from breaking the train of thought. The show must continue, no matter what, and especially if the dialogue and narration are on tape.

It is sometimes difficult to remain calm, but real professionalism emerges when something accidental happens— a puppet's head or leg falling off, strings getting tangled, or the myriad other catastrophes that can occur. Remember, keep cool, and go on with the show!

Music in Puppetry

Music is an important part of your puppet production. Whether you use live or recorded music, you should plan carefully to use some kind of musical accompaniment with your show. It creates the right atmosphere and bridges the gap between the scenes. It can be used to change the mood during acts, as background for action, and as rhythm for dances or pantomimes.

The musical interludes should never be so long as to slow down the action of your play. They should serve as background and never become overpowering or get in the way of the words or action.

Usually you should use music that fits the size of the puppet stage—small musical groups or single instruments like piano, guitar, or recorder. Music boxes or recordings of them are ideal. Sometimes orchestra suites or music from ballets are especially suitable. It depends on the mood or effect you want for your production. To summarize, remember that music should be used in your productions for the following reasons:

(1) Mood—to help bring out the emotional feeling or atmosphere of your play. Ask yourself, is it a happy play, a sad story, a fast-moving story, a silly play, or a serious one? Will the music help or detract from the play? How much music should be used?

(2) Bridges—the music you play while changing scenery. You mustn't let your audience grow restless while you change the scenery or when the action lags.

(3) Songs or dances—try to find just the right dance or song accompaniment for the style of your show. Perhaps children's songs, new or old, might be just right for your

story, even though you might have to change the lyrics to fit the action.

(4) Background—sometimes added music will enhance the action, as when the story is spooky or sad.

(5) Opening music—to get your show off to a good start.

Below are some suggestions for recordings or musical ideas you might wish to try for the plays in this book. Most of them are popular enough to be found in your local record stores. The record dealer may also be able to give you some suggestions, if you tell him the type of mood you are trying to achieve in the play.

Pinocchio—Neapolitan Mandolins, RCA Victor FSP-115

*The Tinderbox—*Symphony No. 3, *"Ilya Murometz,"* Glière (several recordings)

The Magic Mushrooms—Piano Music for Children, Kabalevsky MGM E3322

The Frog Prince—Bird Fancier's Delight, VOX PL 12-750

Jack and the Beanstalk—Modern Times (movie sound track) UAL 4049

The Princess and the Pea—Ancient Airs and Dances, Respighi, Mercury MG 90199

The Magic Shoes—German Dances, VOX PL 12-580

Snow White and the Seven Dwarfs—Wood Dove & Golden Spinning Wheel, Artia, ALP 200

Alice's Adventures in Wonderland—All in a Garden Green, Counterpoint/Esoteric M-2658-616

The Wizard of Oz—La Boutique Fantasque, Rossini/Respighi (several recordings)

Why the Sea Is Salt—Piano Music for Children, MGM E3010

The Reluctant Dragon—Symphonies and Fanfares for the King's Supper, Nonesuch H-71009

You may use live music, if there is someone in your group who plays the piano, guitar, or recorder (or even simple instruments such as the mouth organ, or paper-over-comb). You may wish to add other instruments such as tambourines, rhythm sticks, bells or drums. Be original and create your own moods with sound!